Absolutely Epic

DOT-TO-DOTS

This edition published in 2022 by Arcturus Publishing Limited
26/27 Bickels Yard, 151–153 Bermondsey Street,
London SE1 3HA

Cover artwork: Luke Seguin-Magee
Interior illustrations: Jo Moon and Shutterstock
Editor: Donna Gregory
Designer: Steve Flight

CH008641NT
Supplier 10, Date 0122, Print run 11443

Printed in the UK

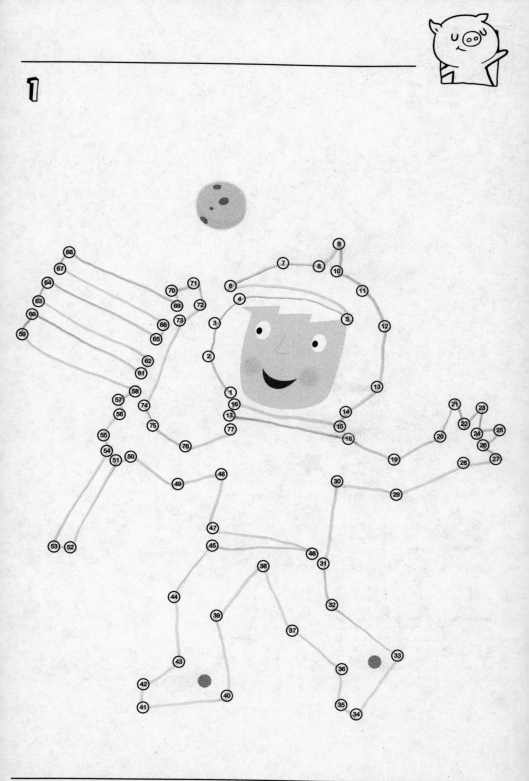

2

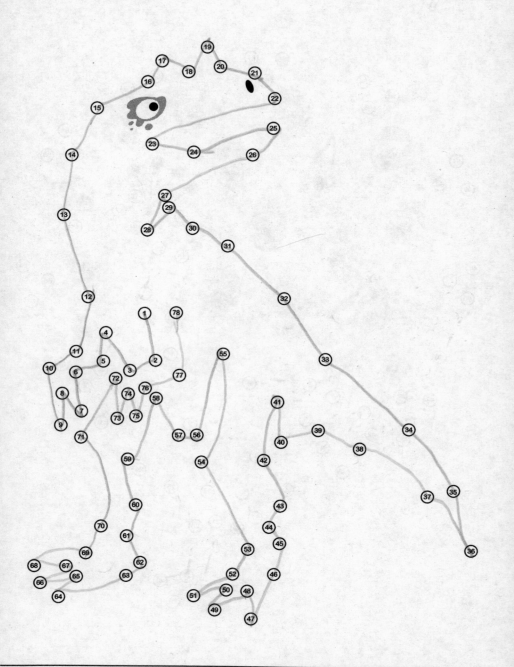

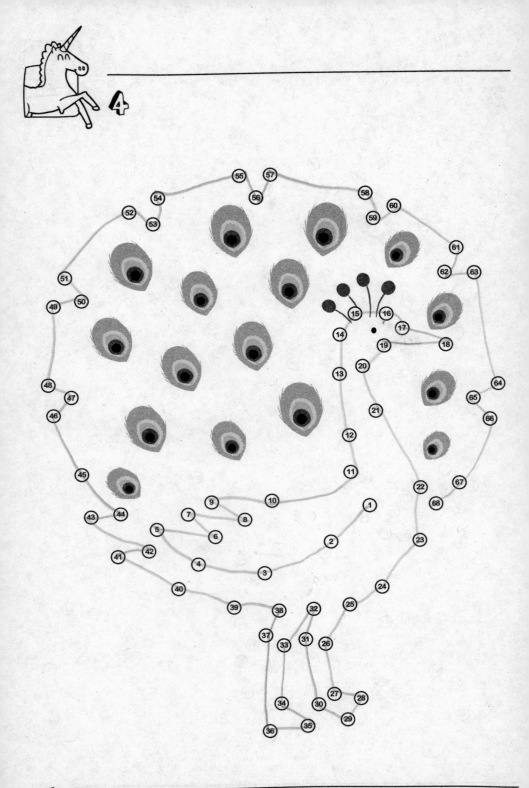

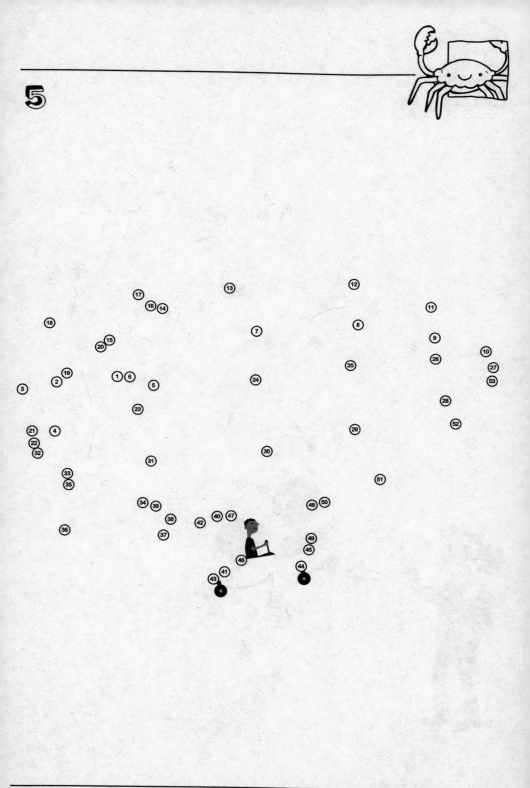

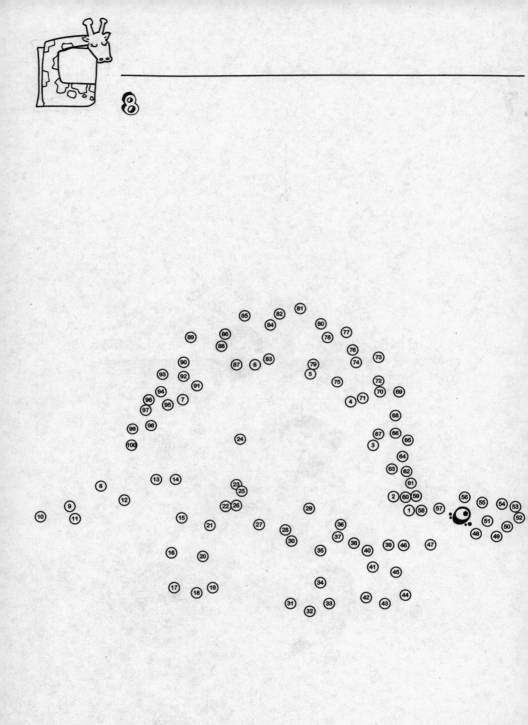

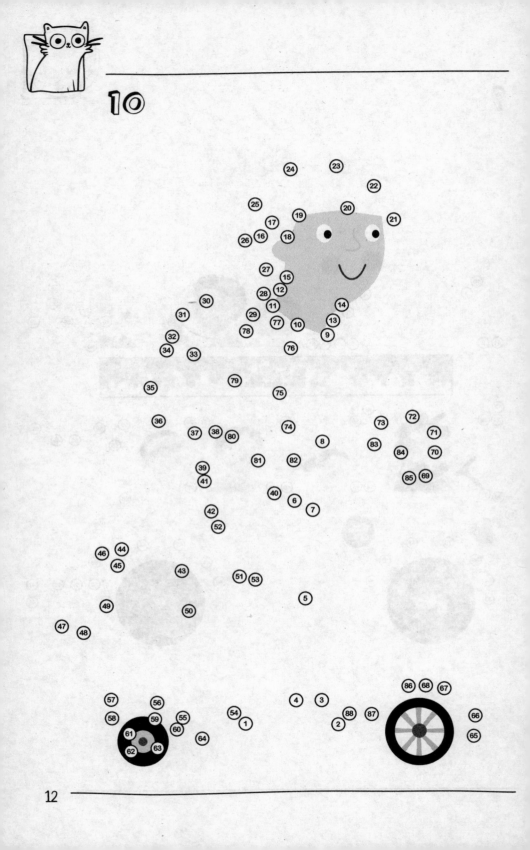

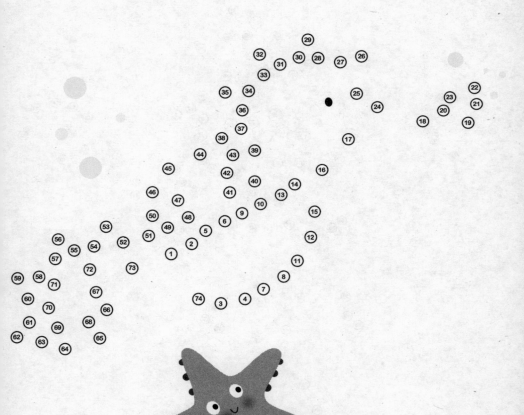

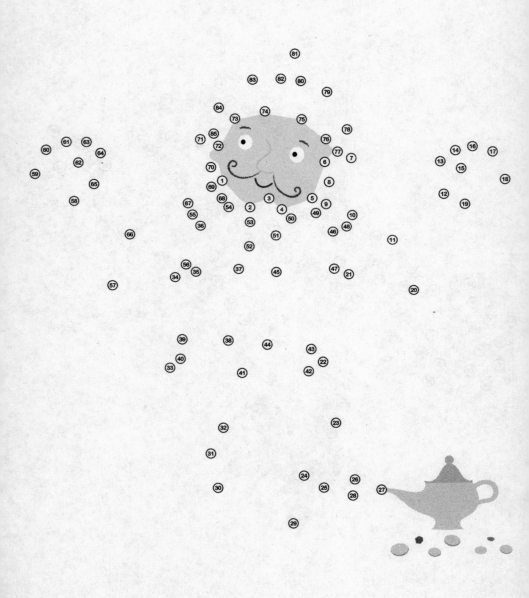

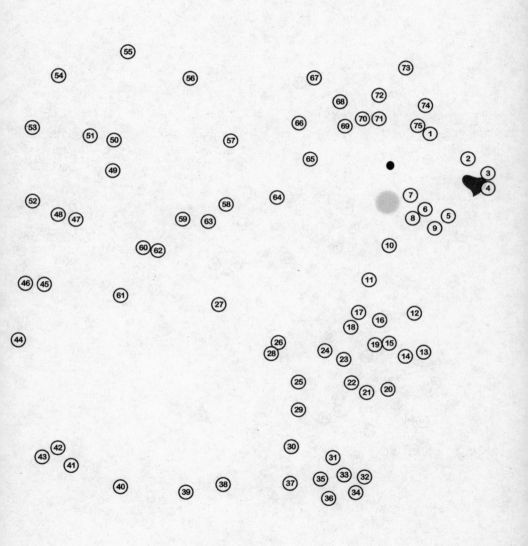

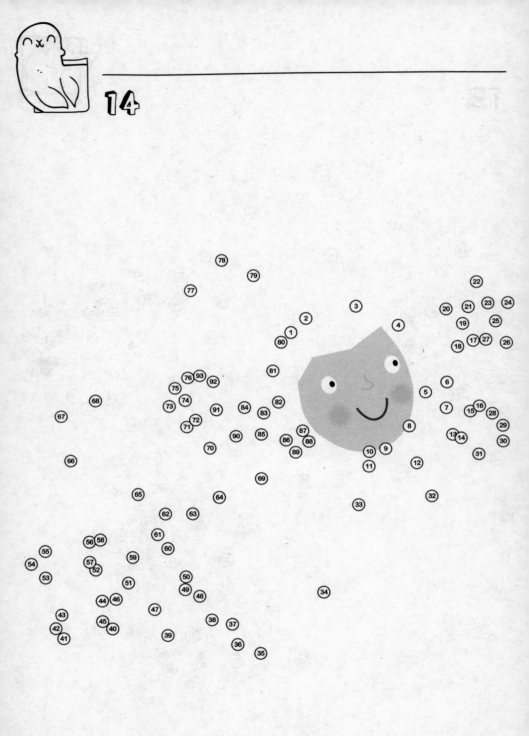

14

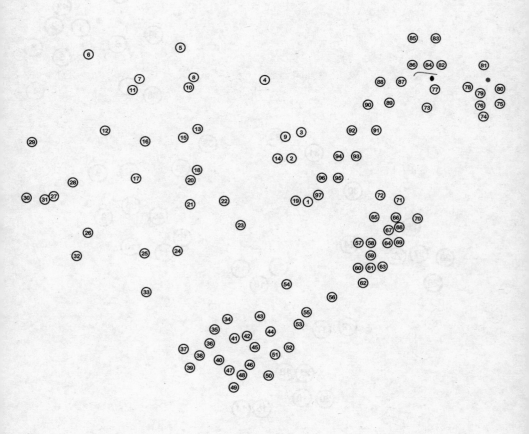

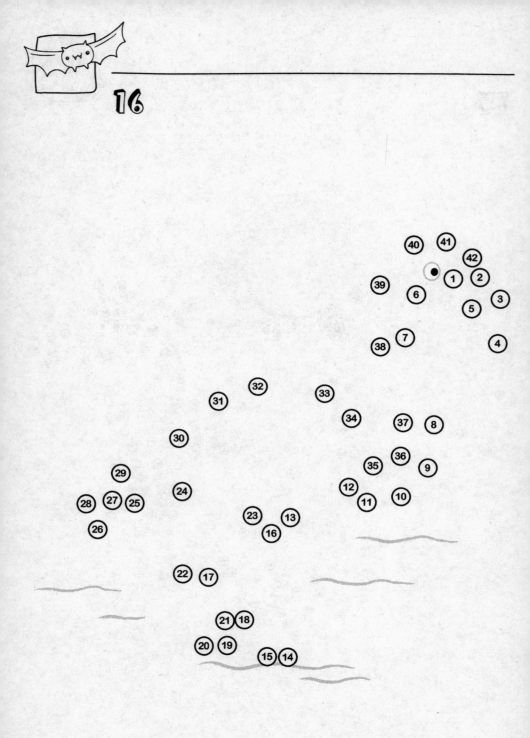

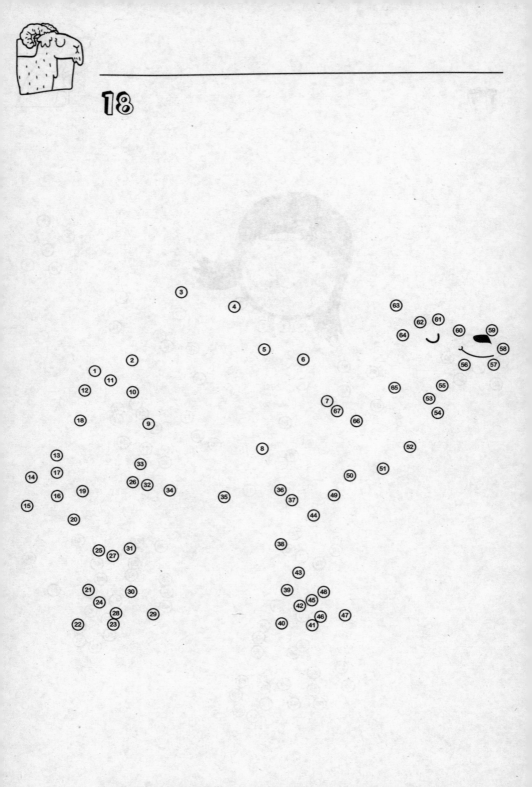

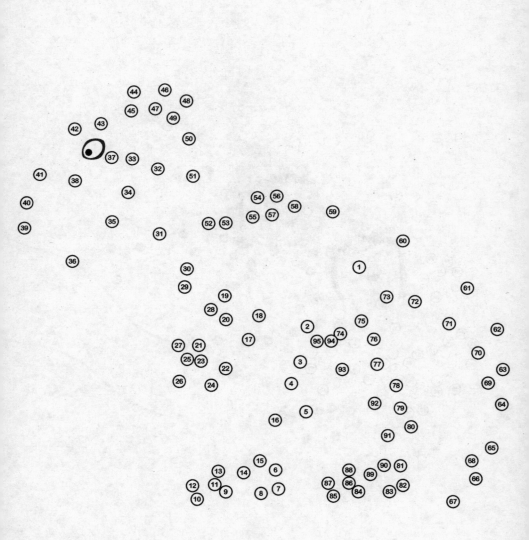

42 43
40 41 44 45
39 46
54 53 52
55 51
56 50
38 47
37 57 49 5
59 58 62 65 48
60 61 63 64 66 67 4
2
36 1 3 6
33 9
35
34 31 7
32 28 8
26 30 10
27 29
23
25 21
17
24 22
19
18 20
16 11
15 12
14 13

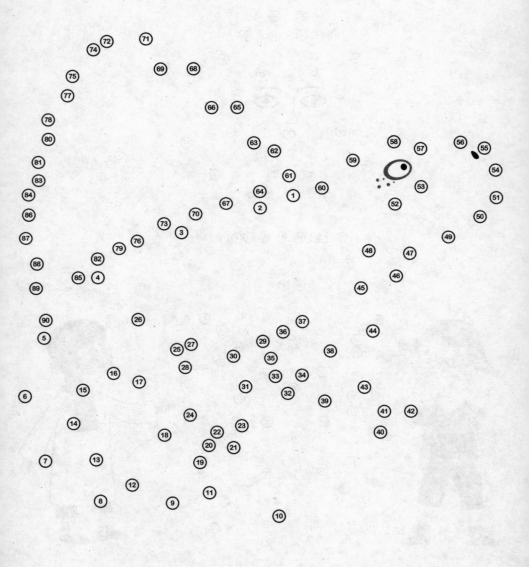

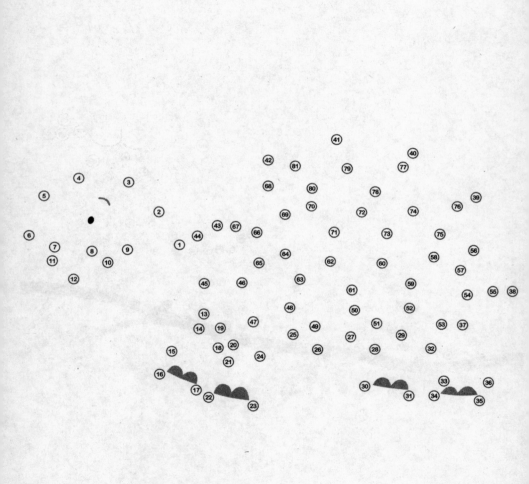

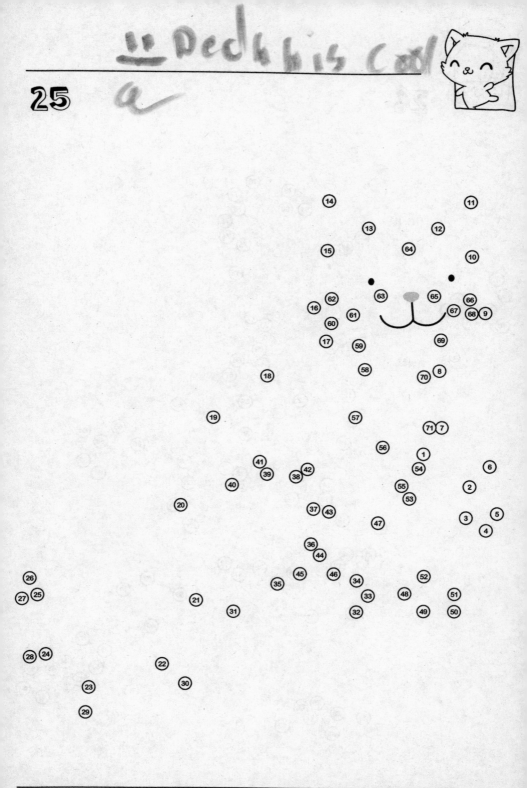

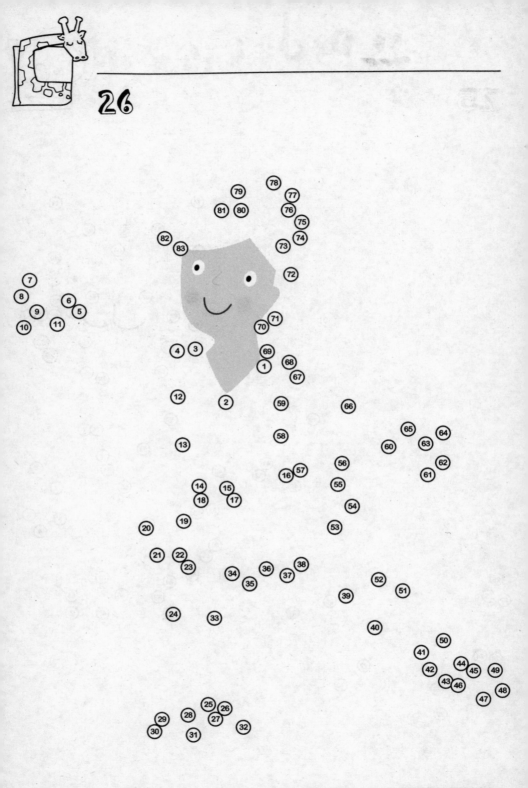

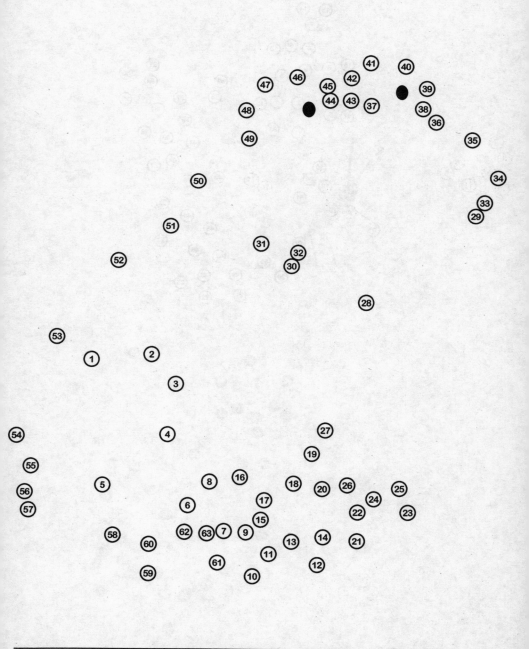

28

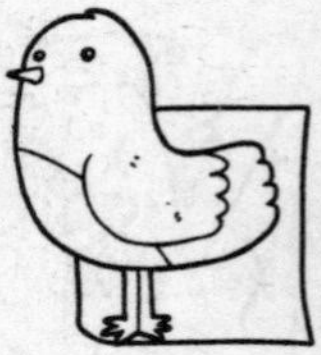

29

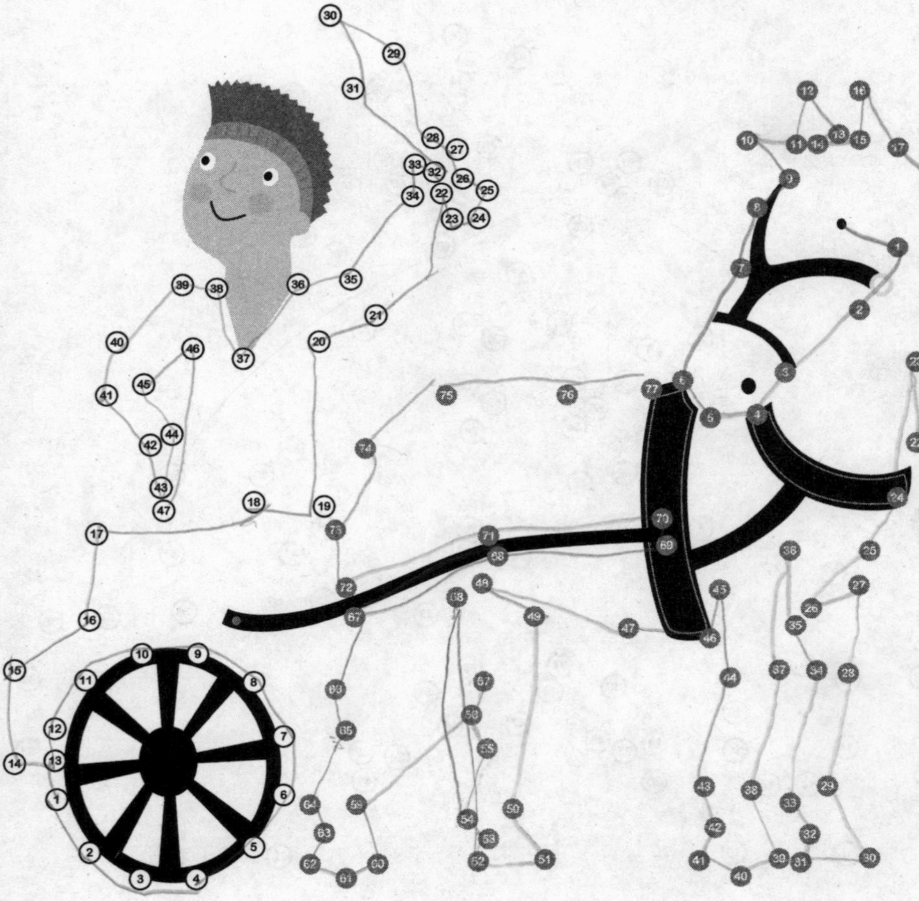

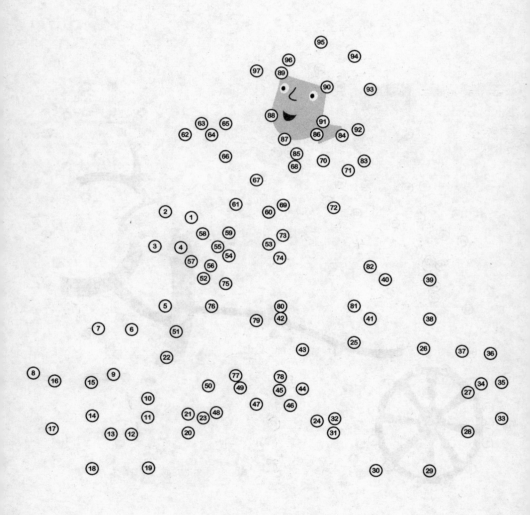

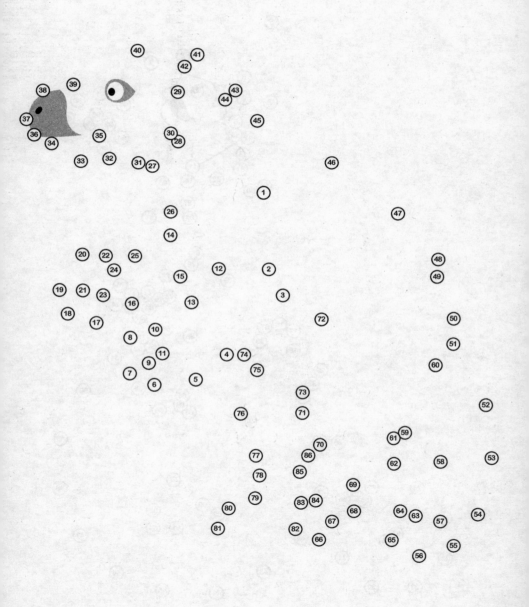

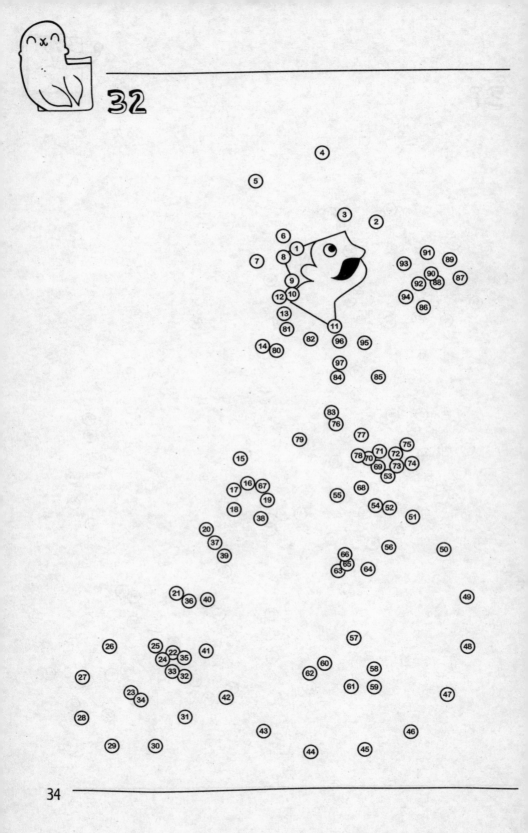

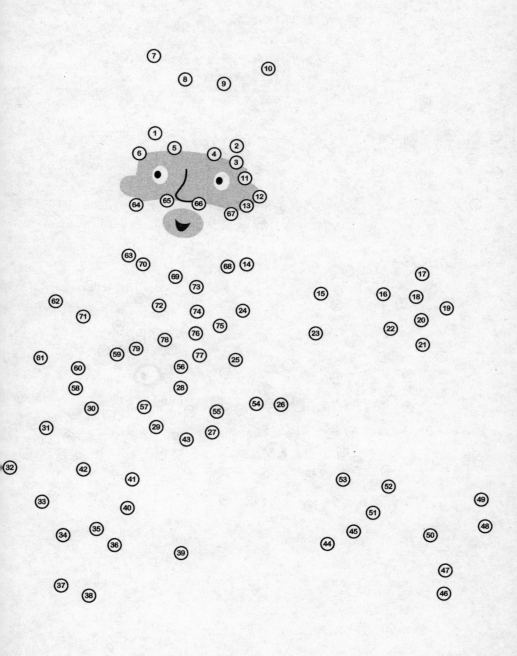

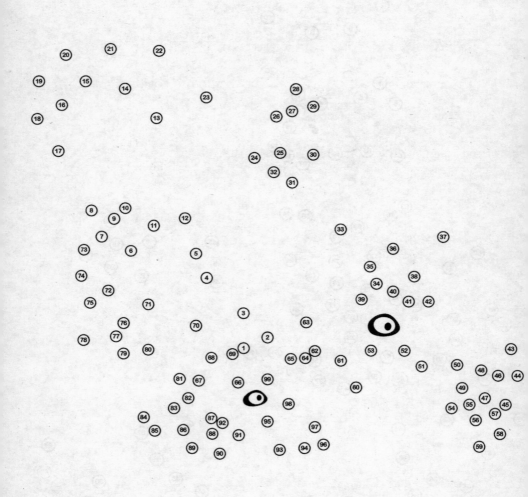

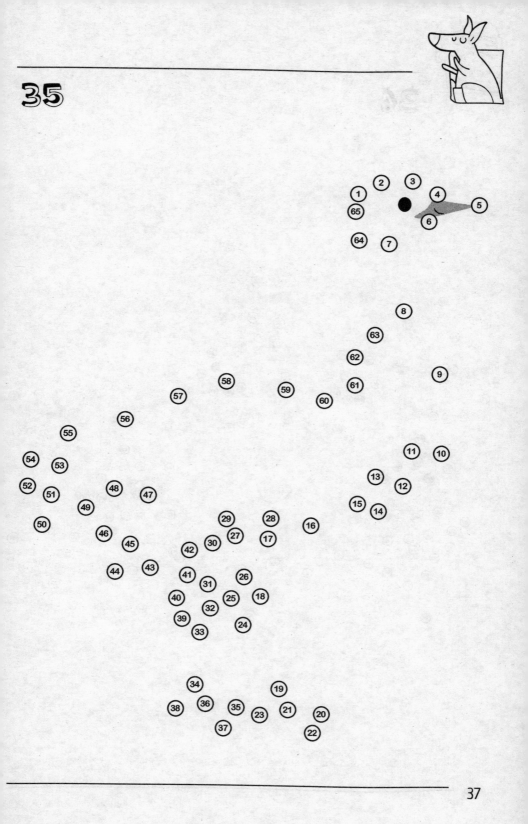

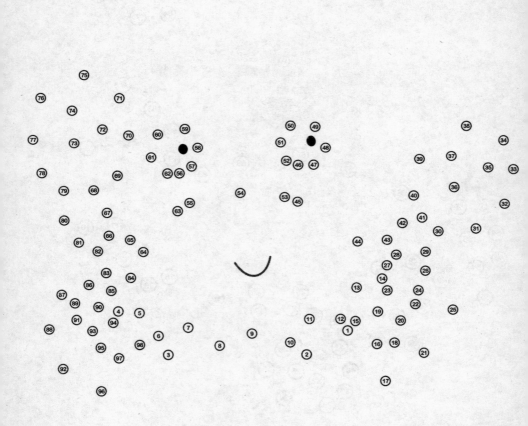

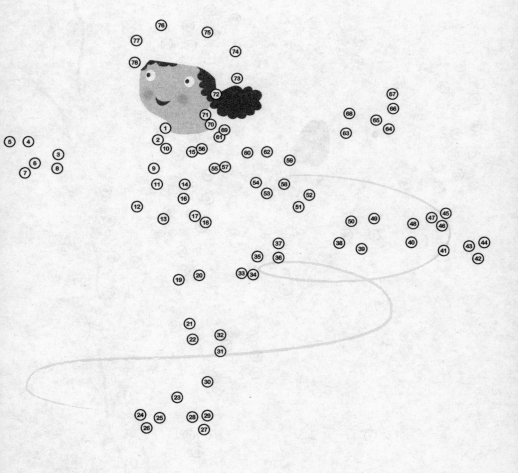

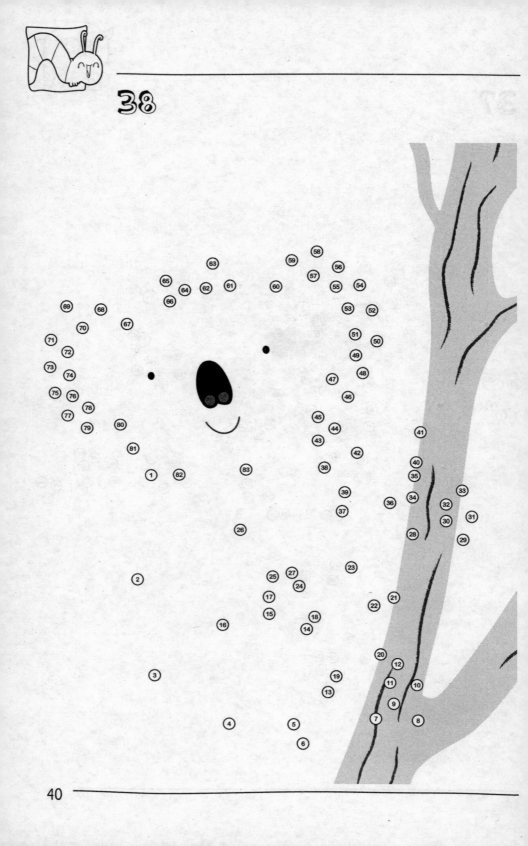

38

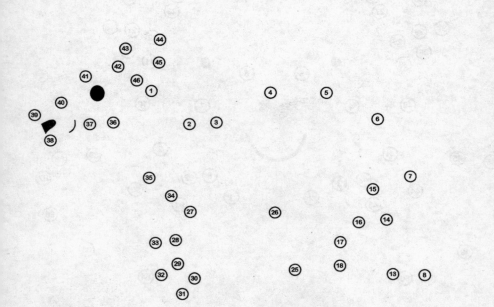

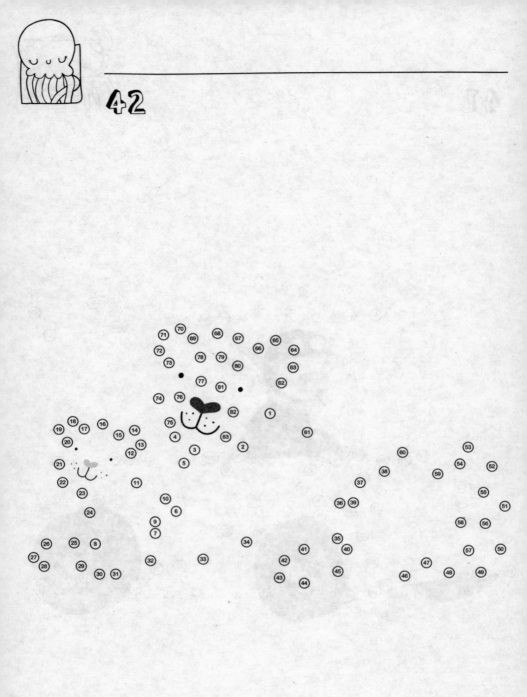

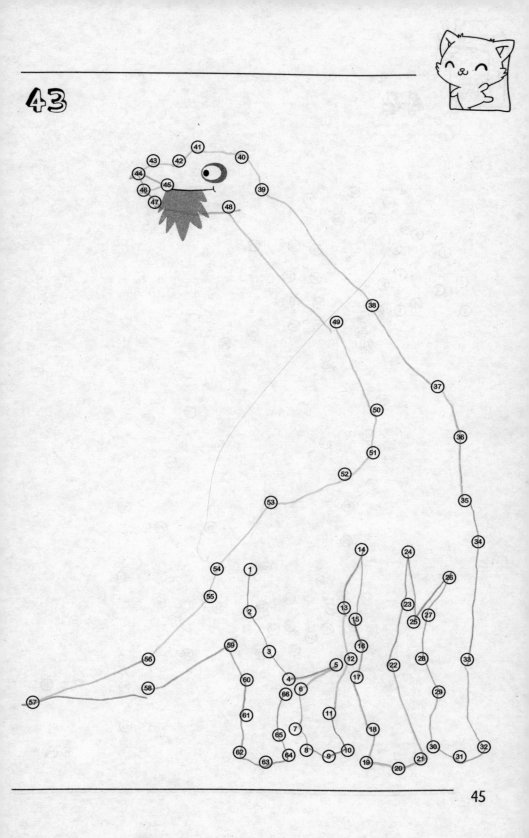

44

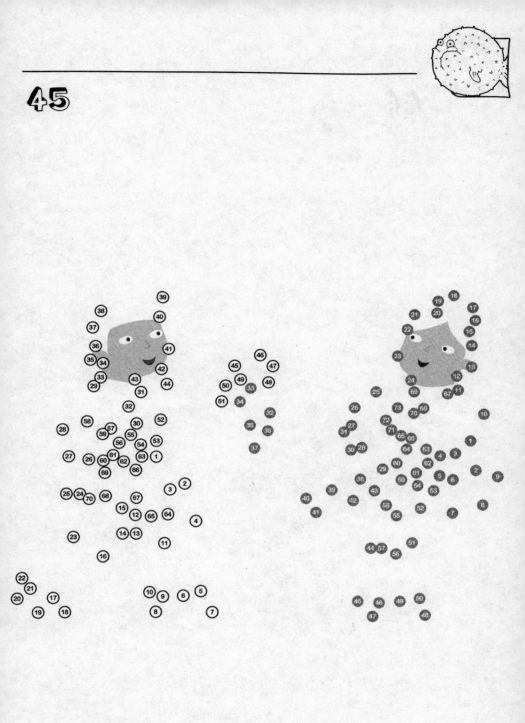

46

48

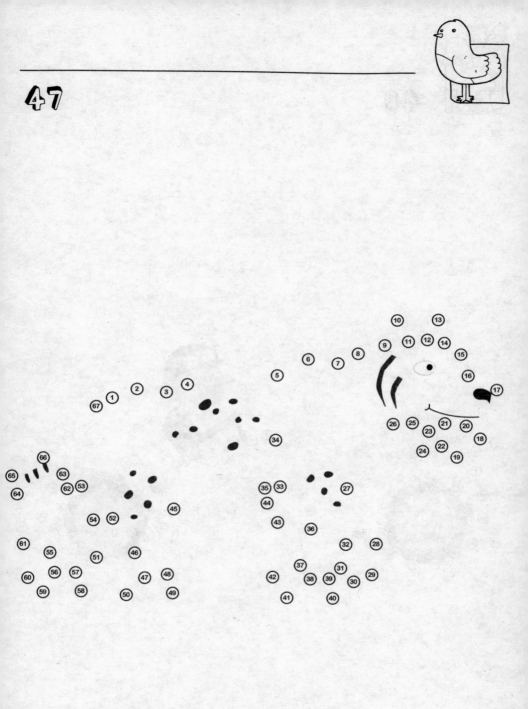

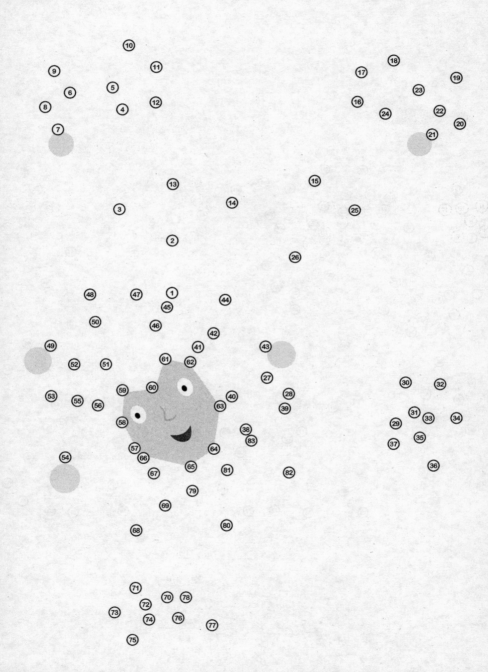

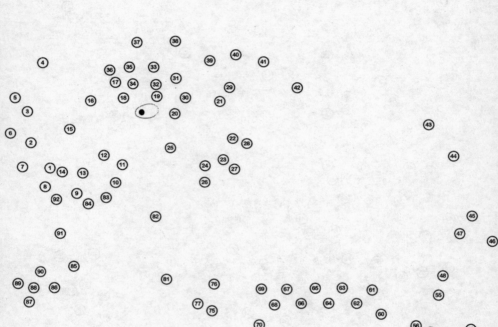

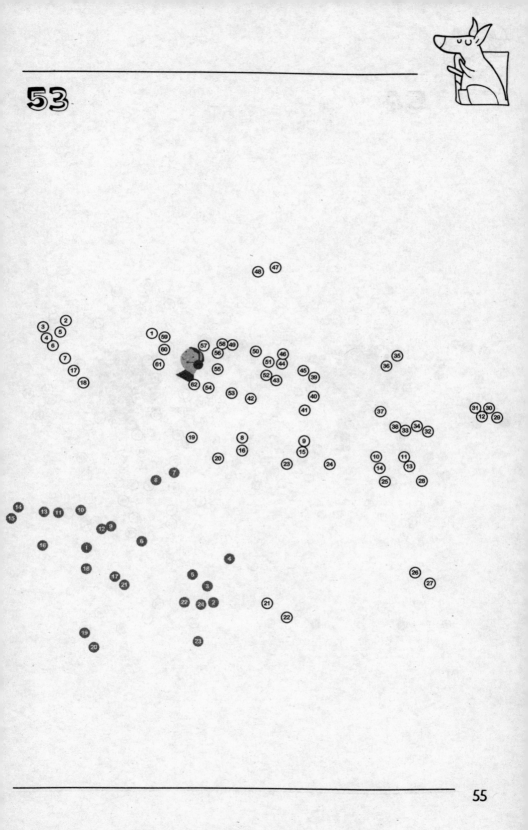

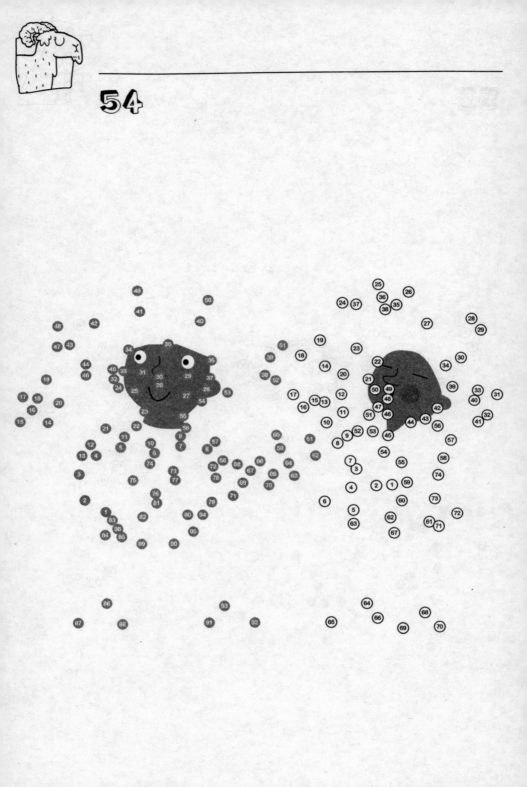

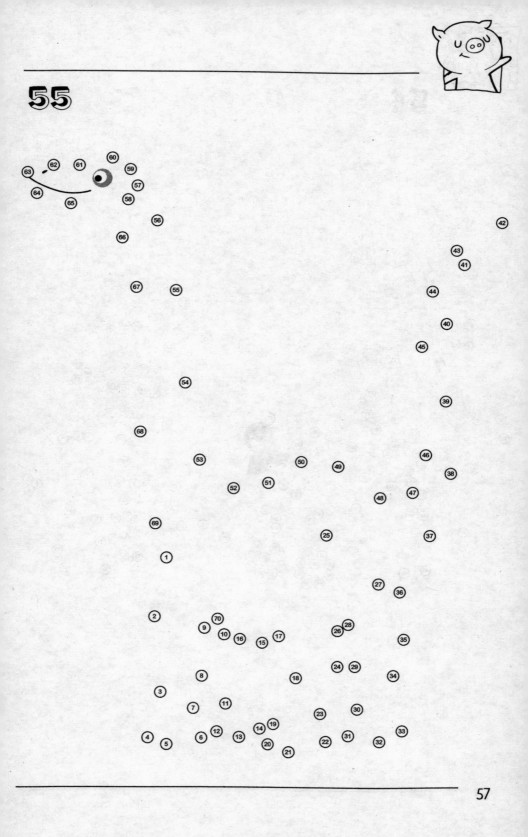

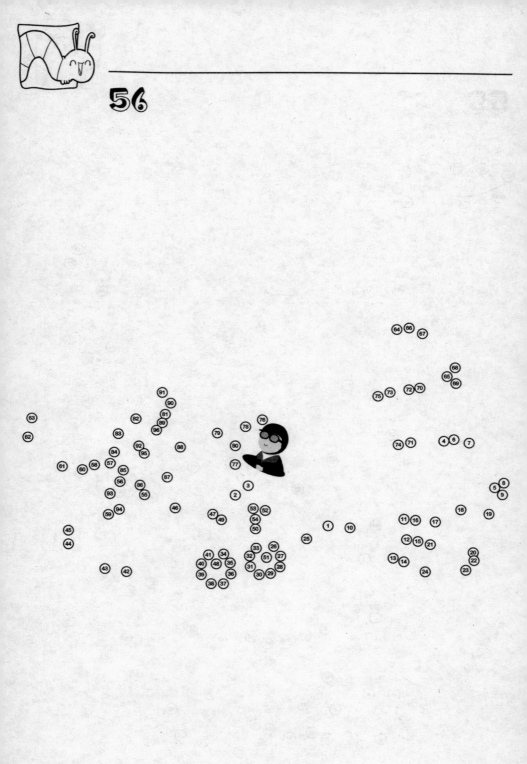

57

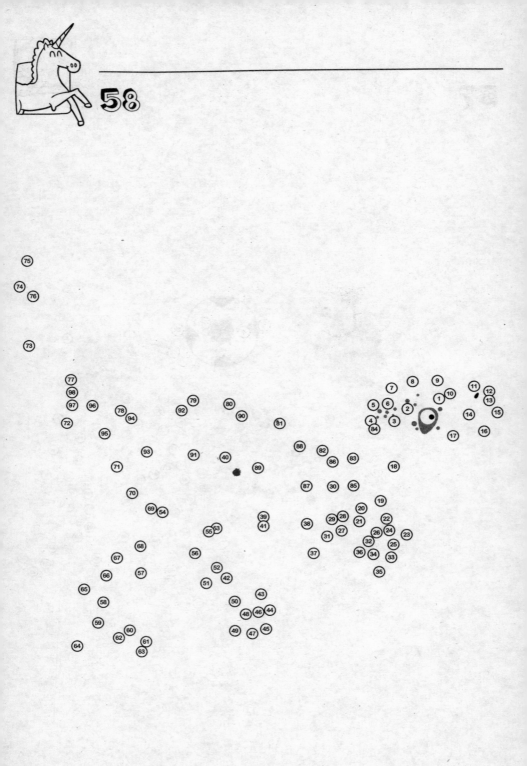

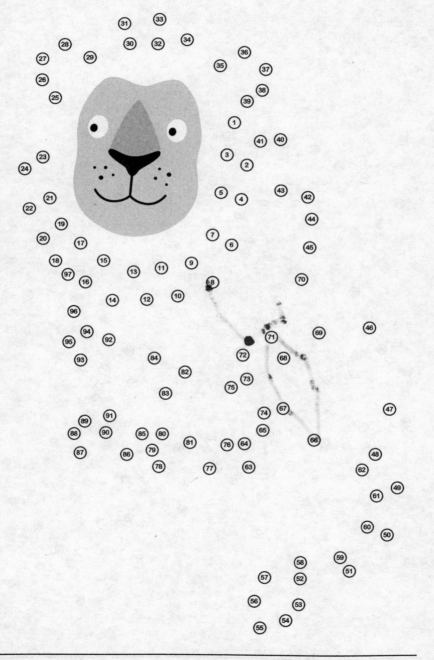

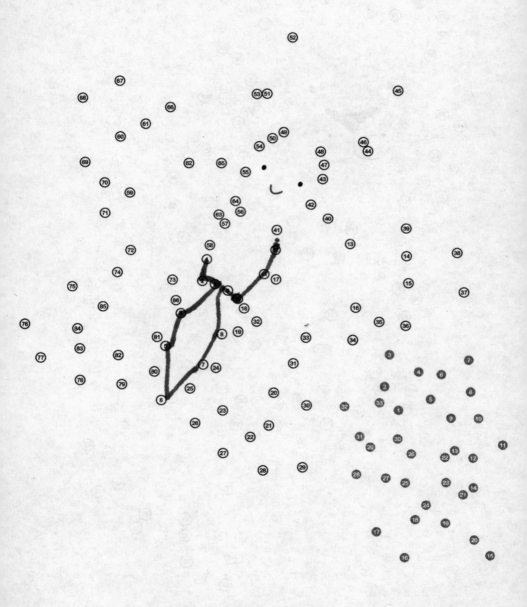

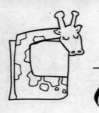

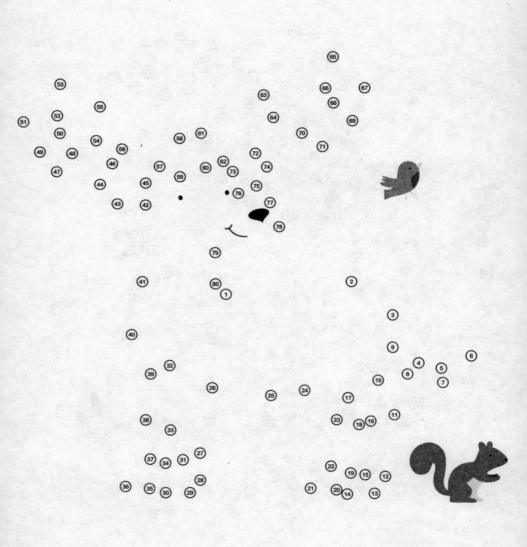

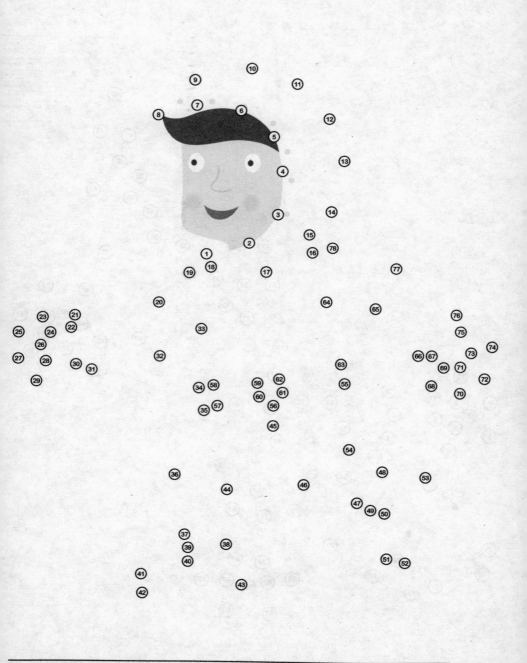

64

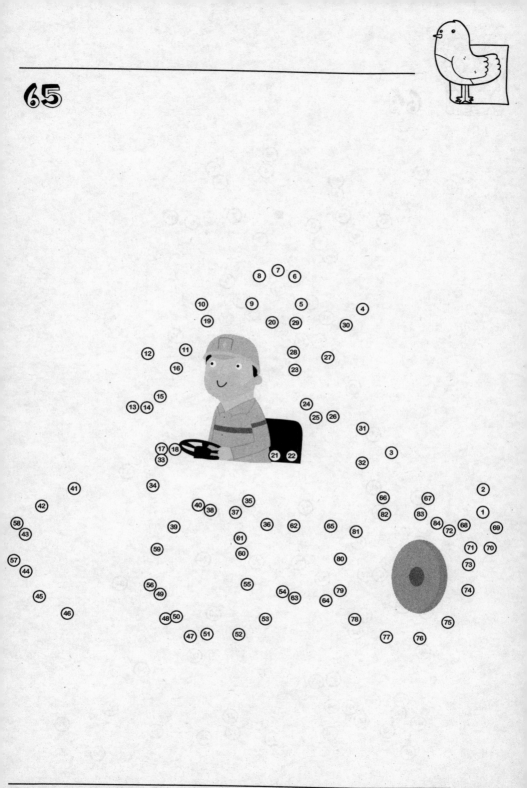

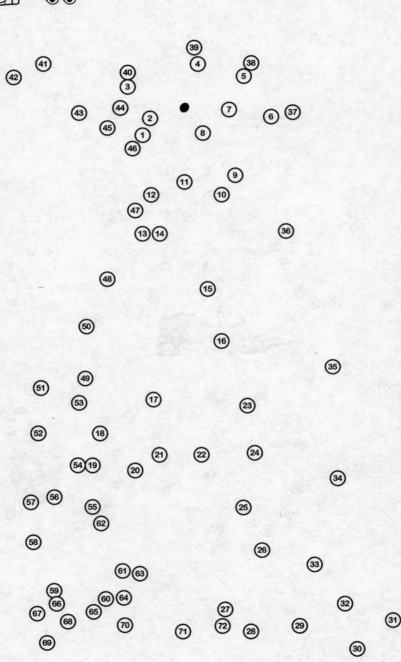

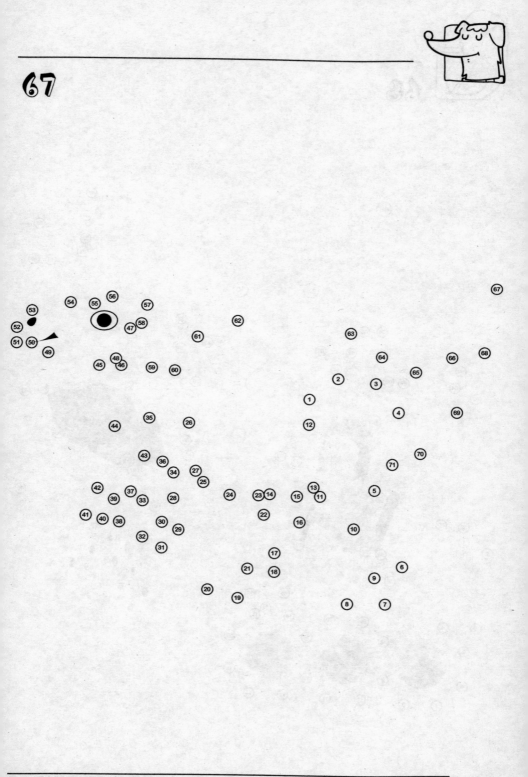

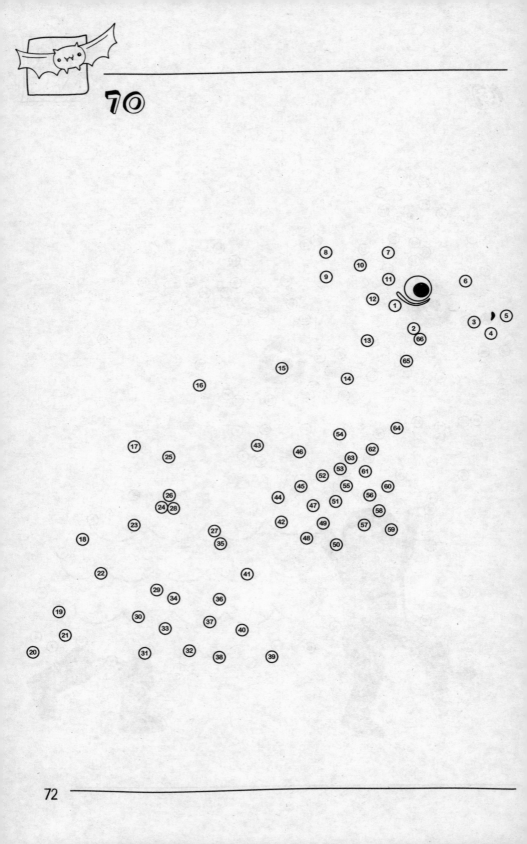

71

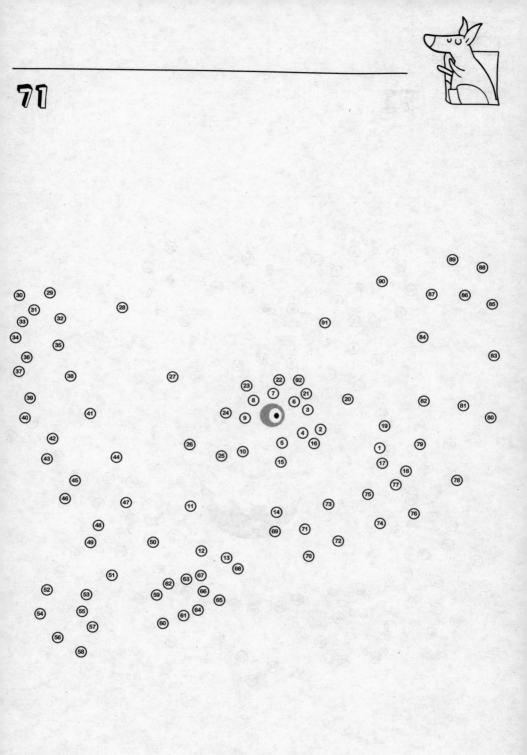

73

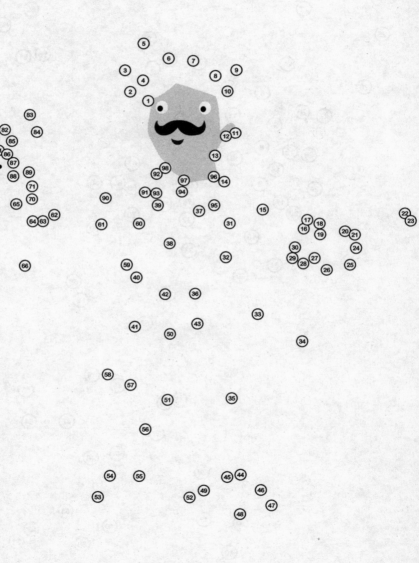

74

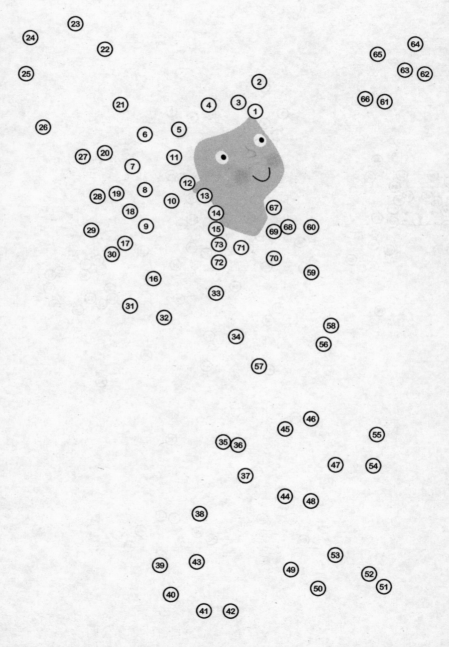

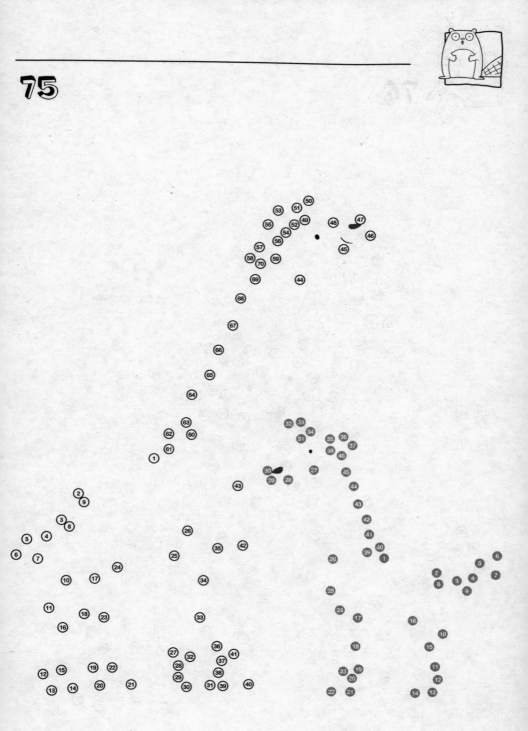

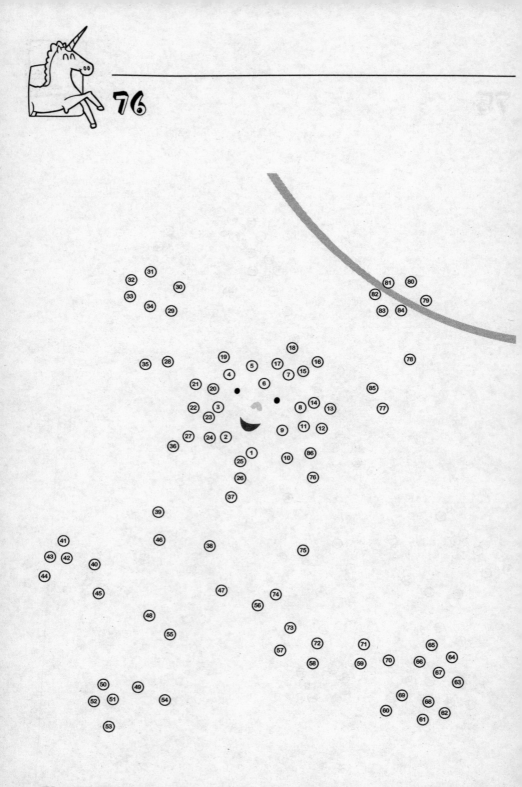

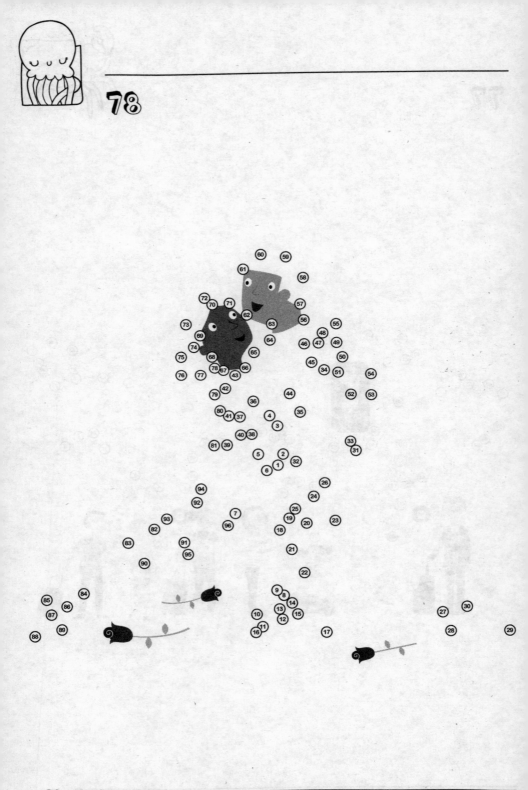

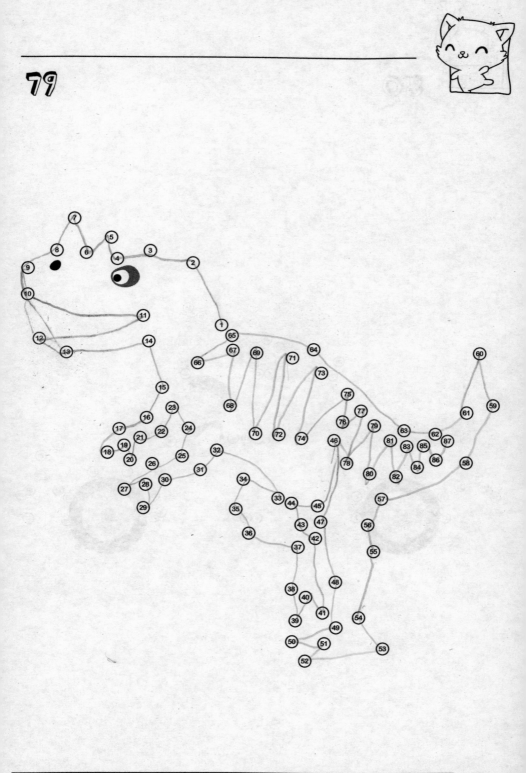

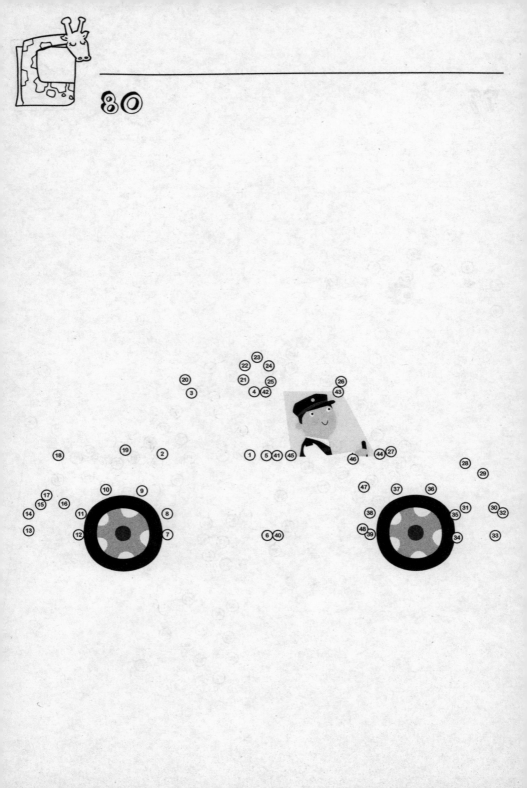

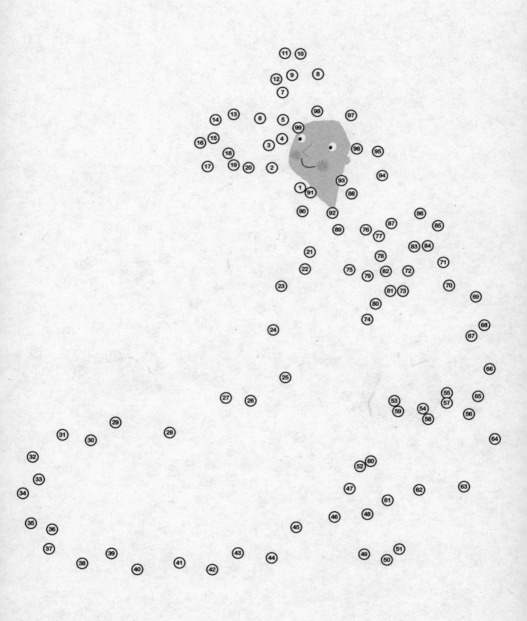

82

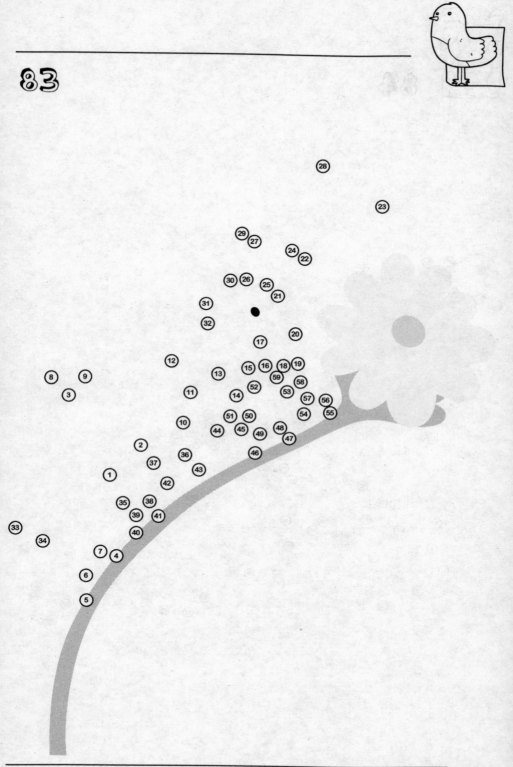

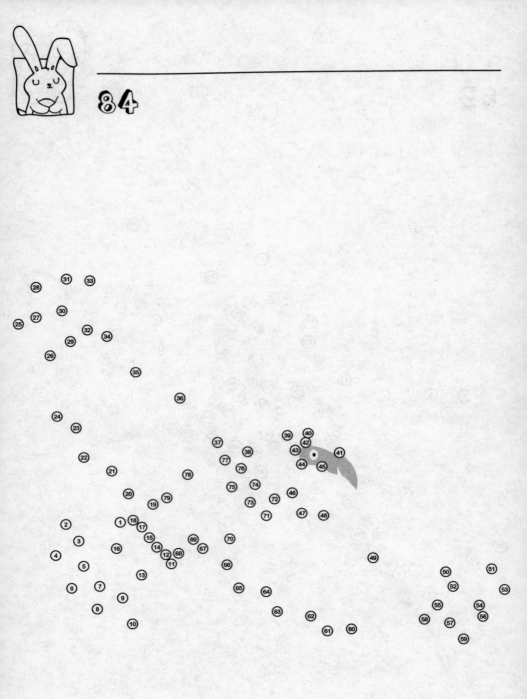

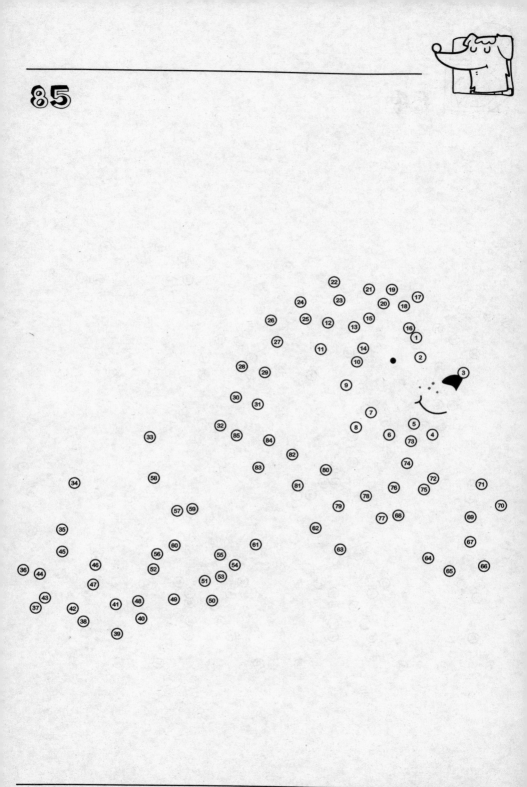

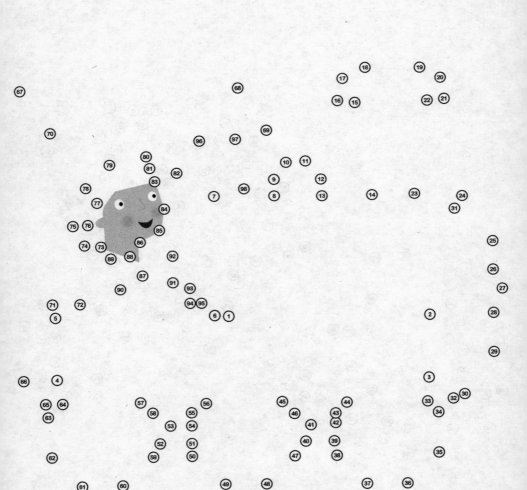

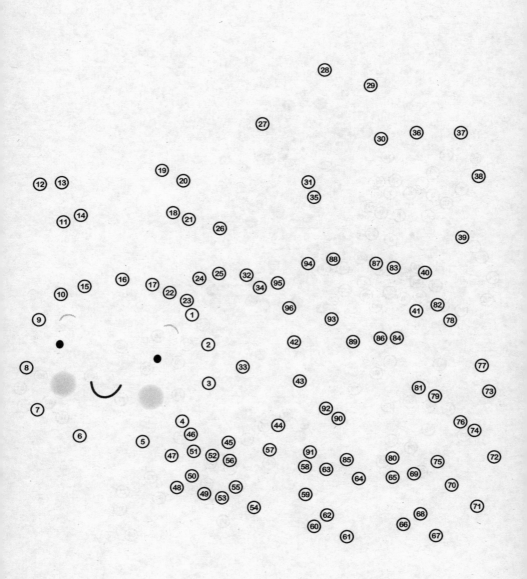

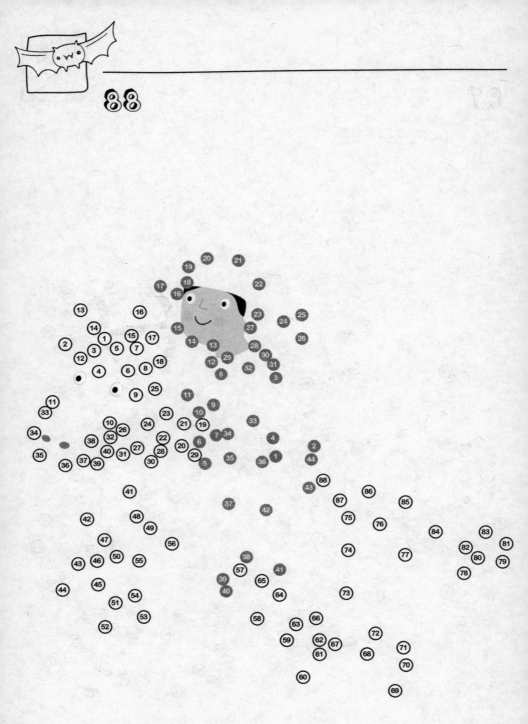

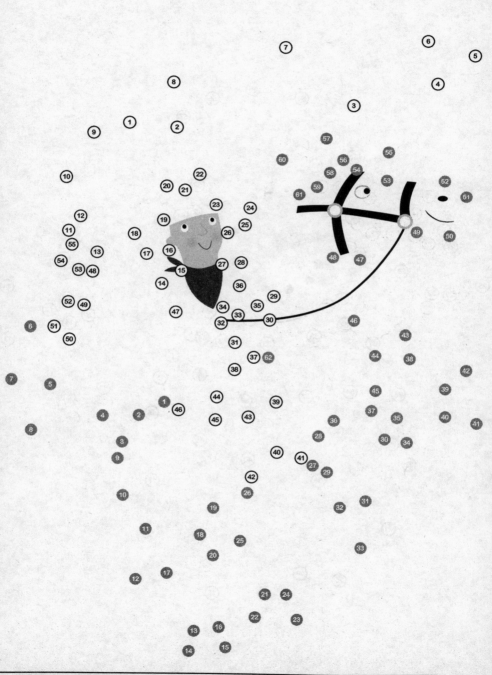

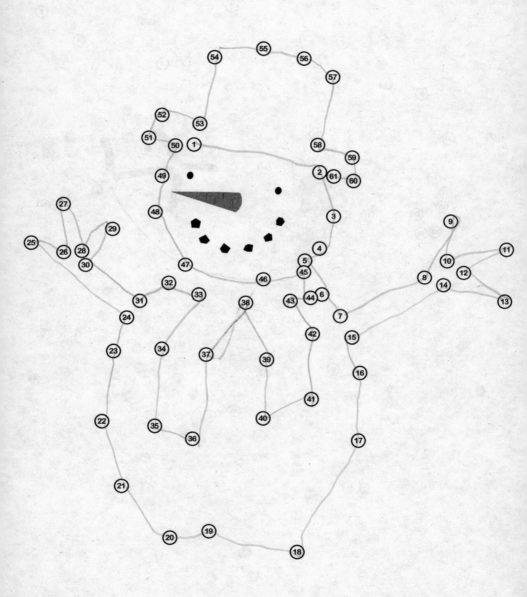

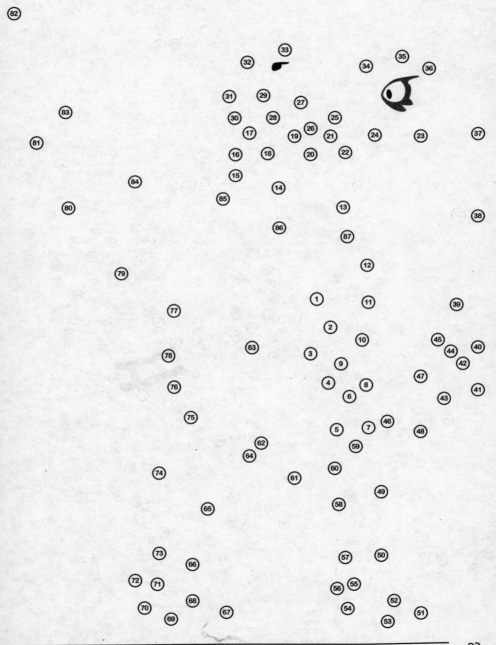

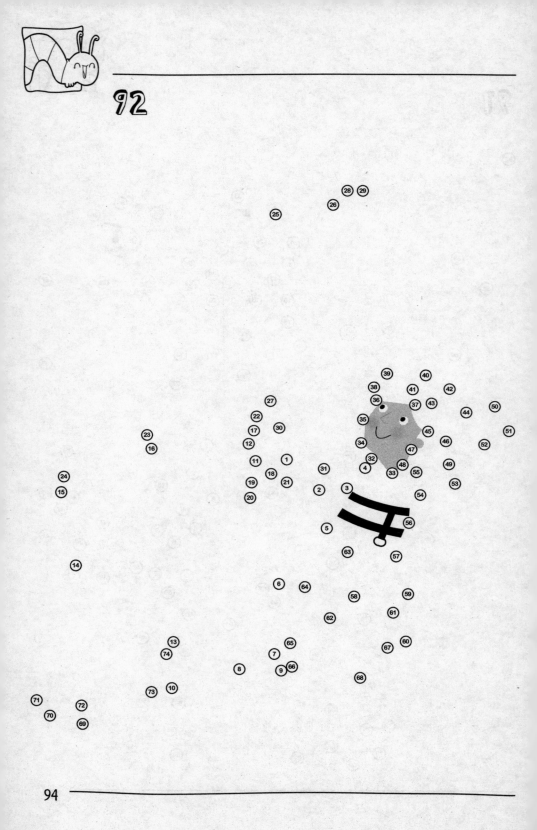

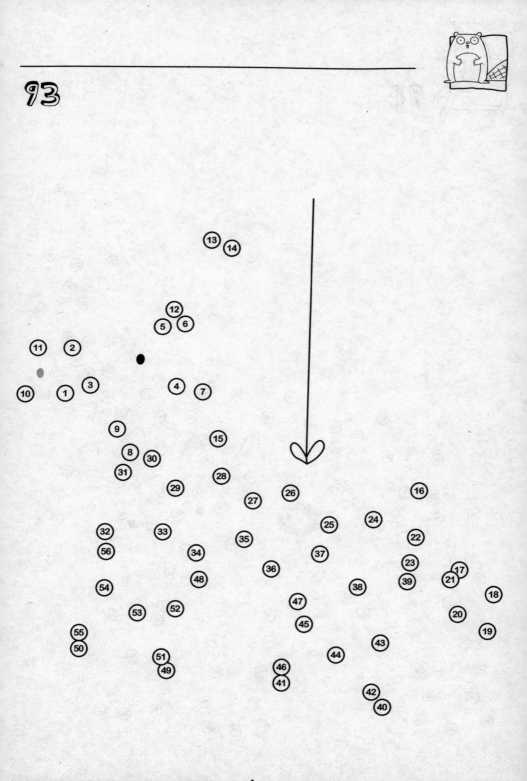

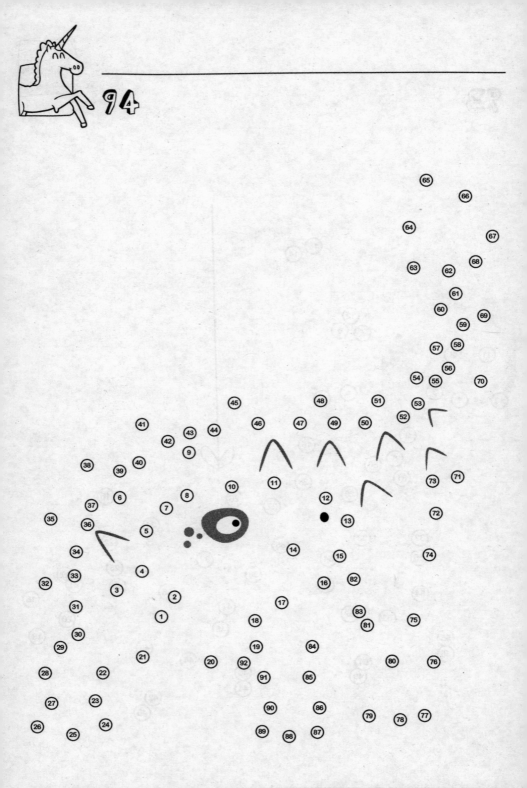

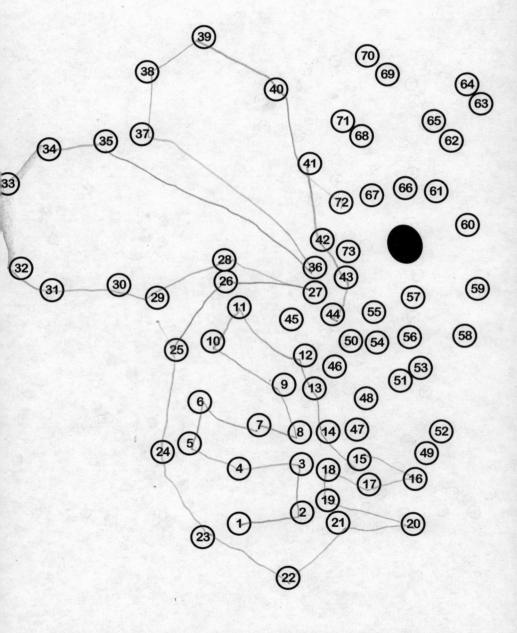

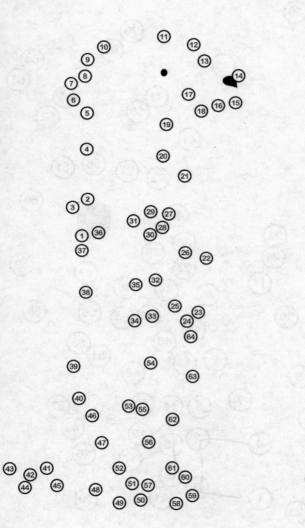

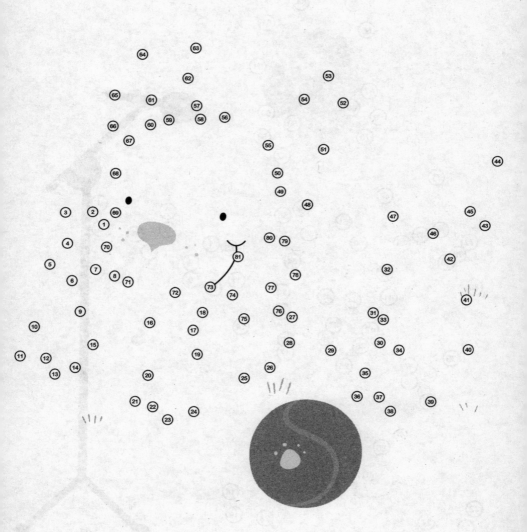

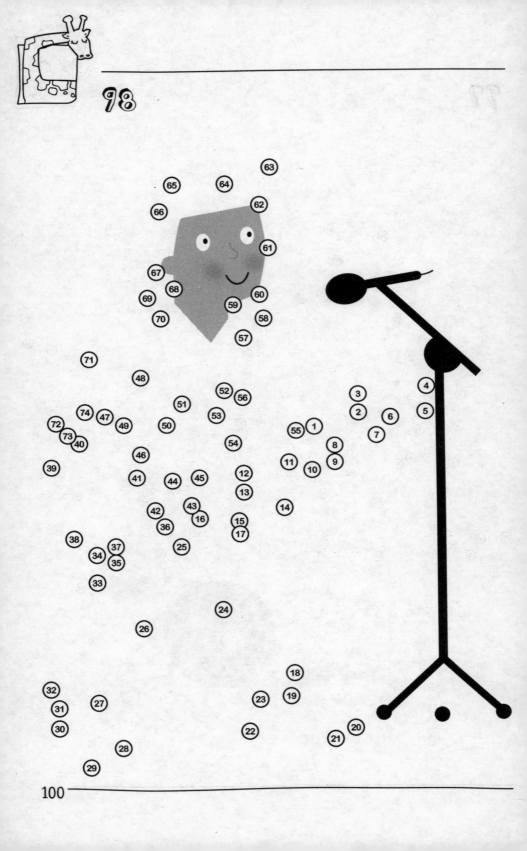

99

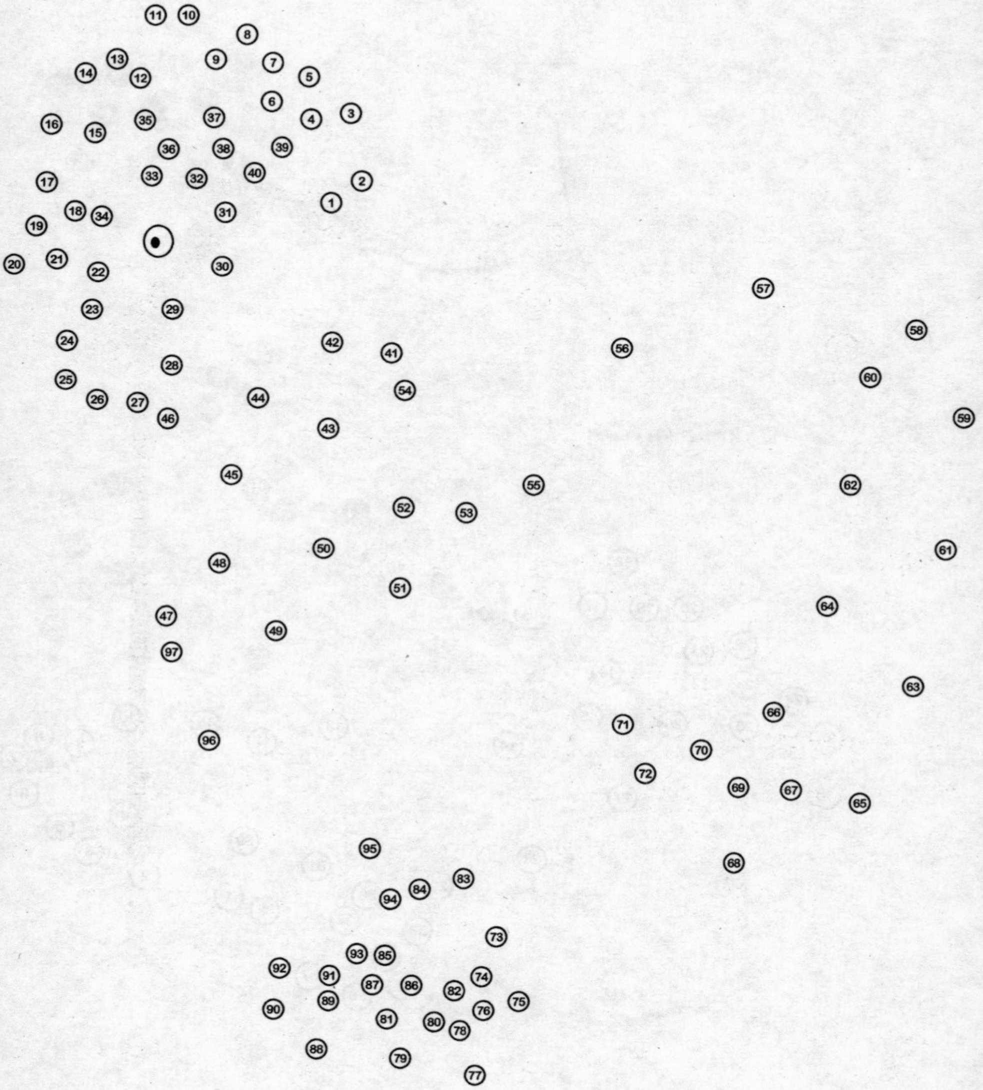

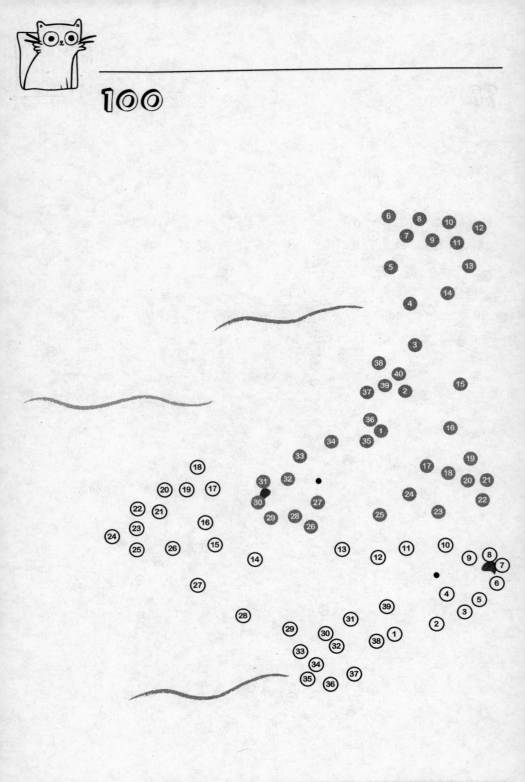

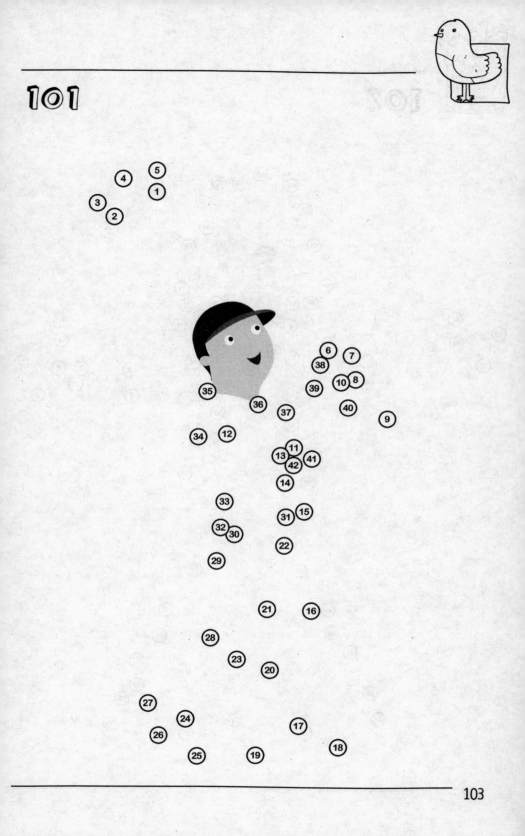

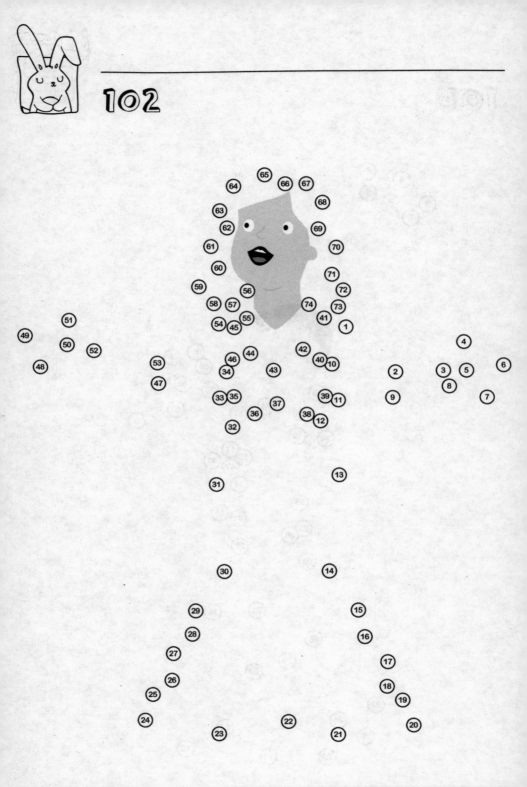

102

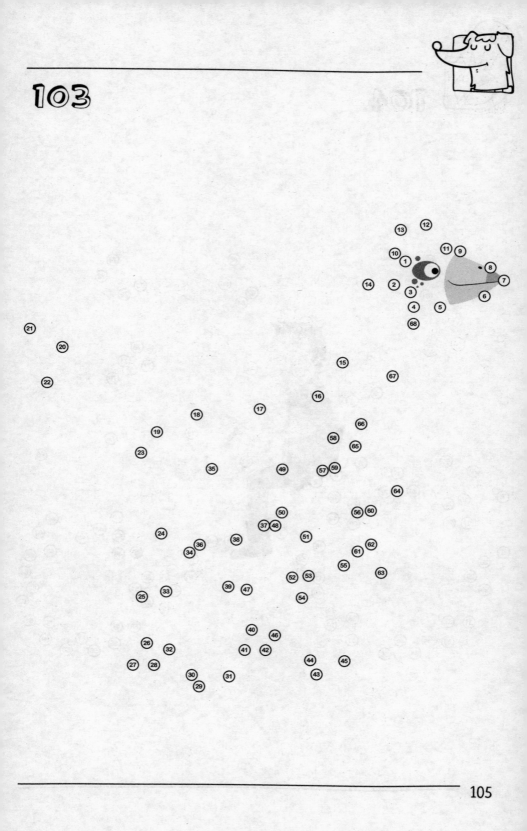

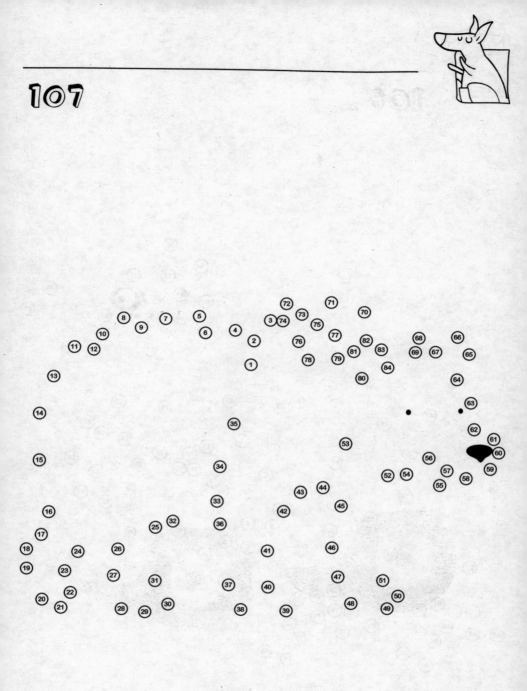

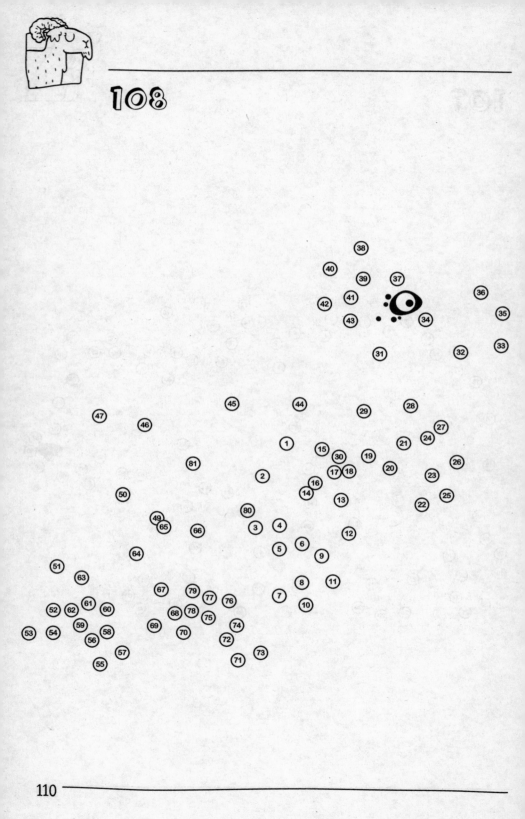

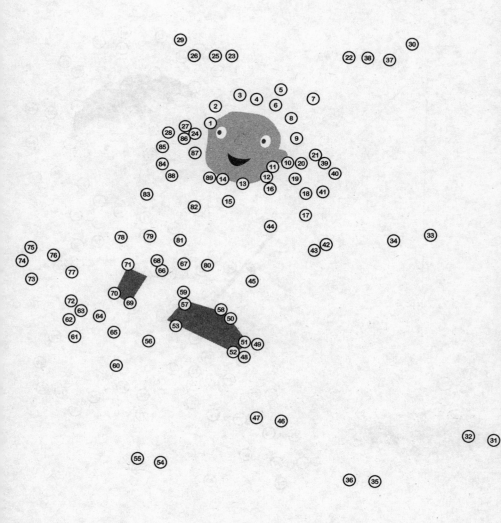

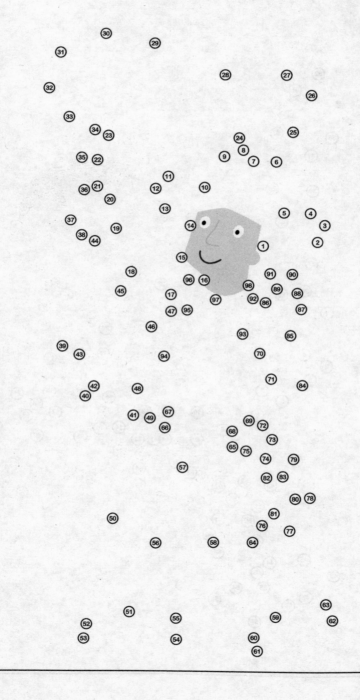

112

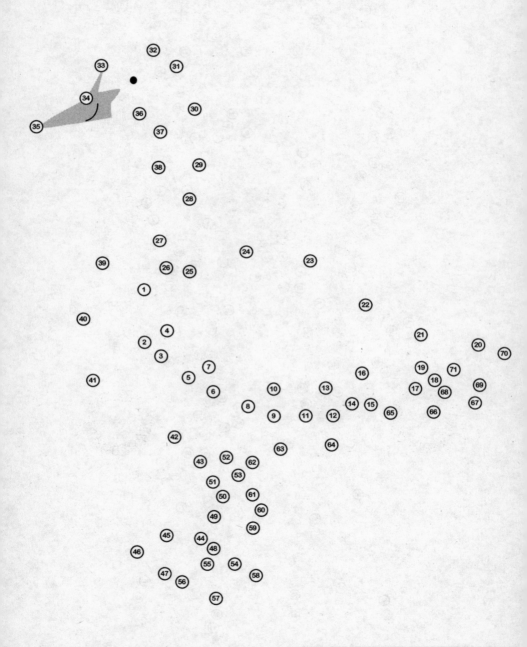

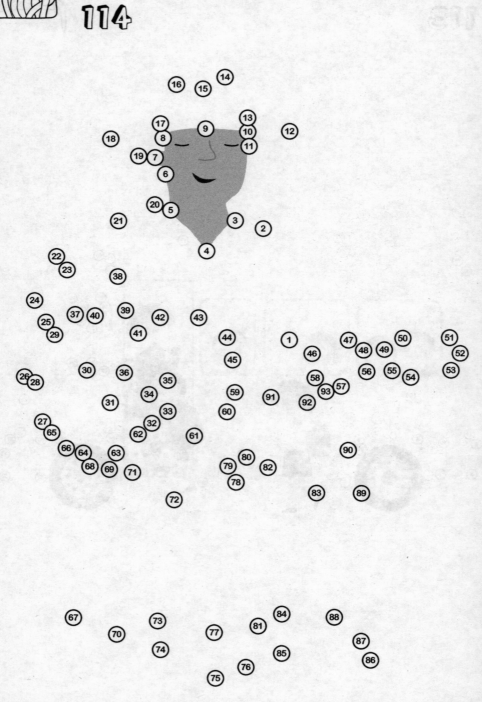

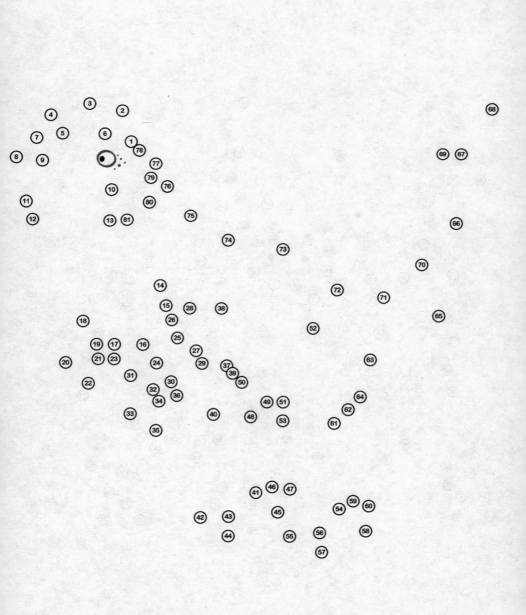

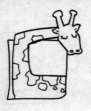

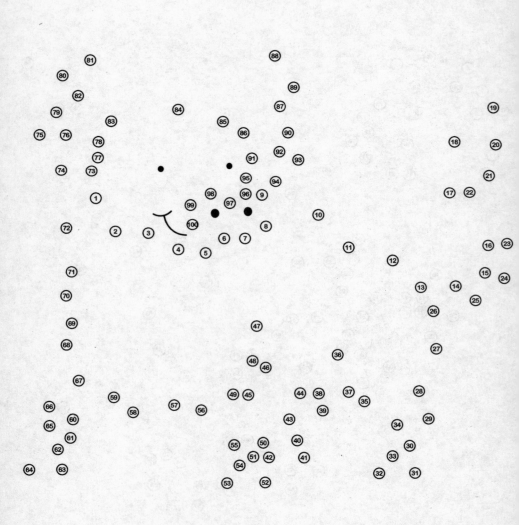

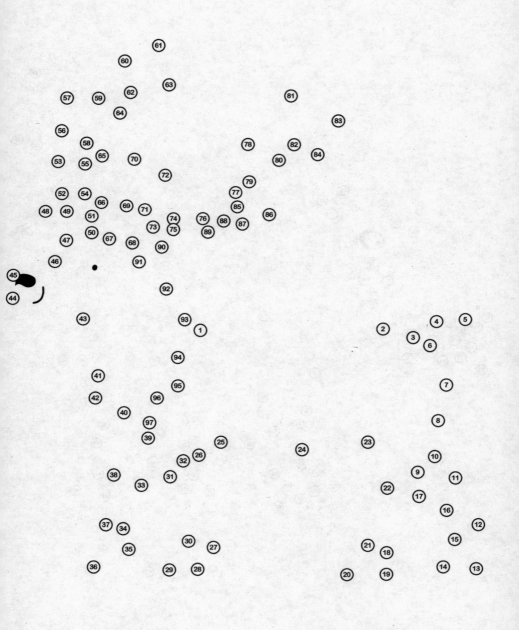

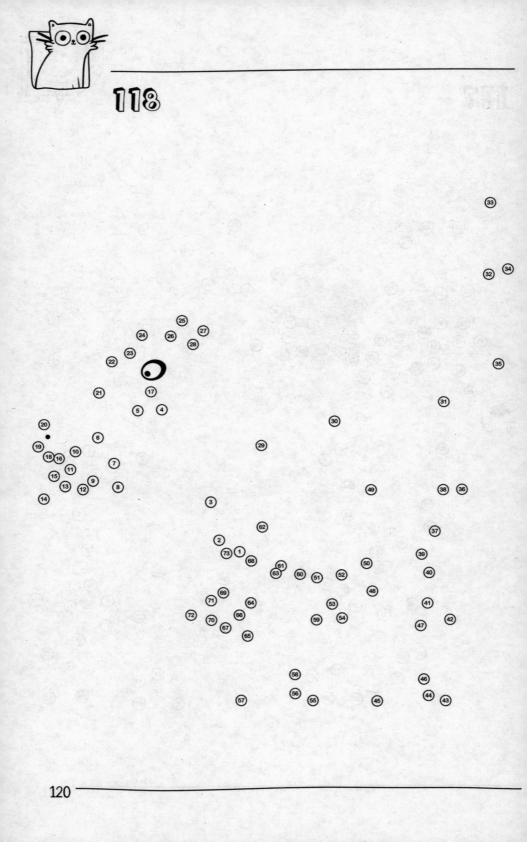

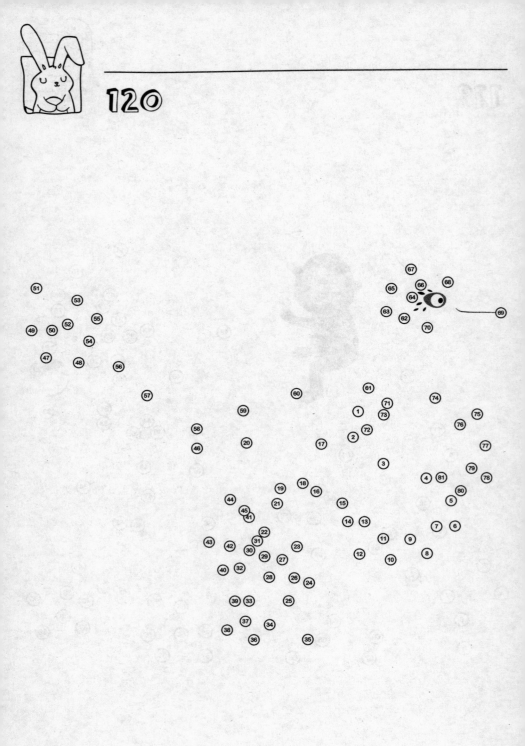

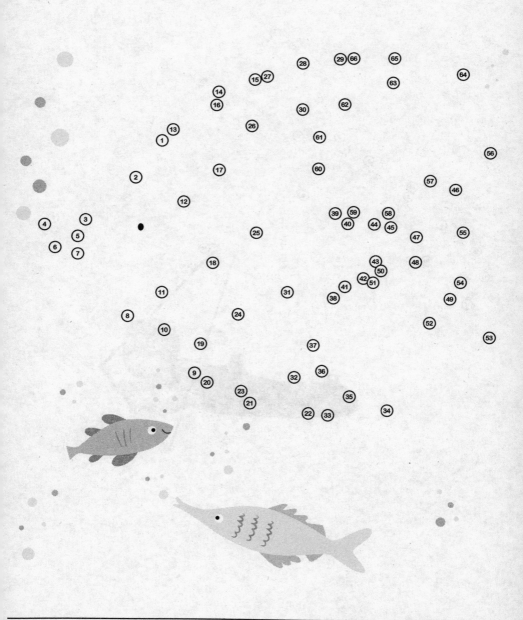

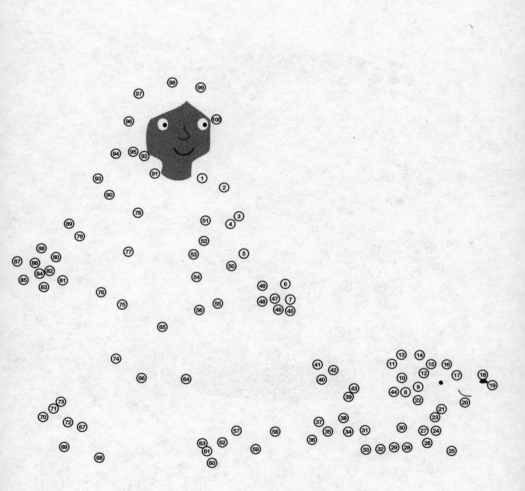

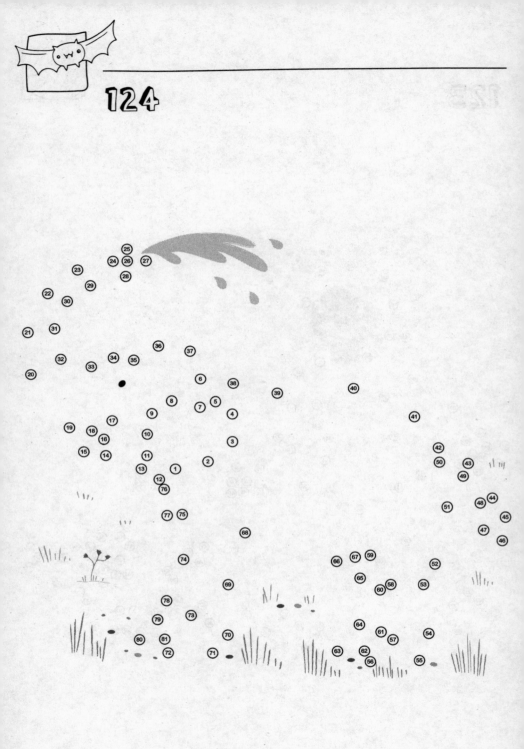

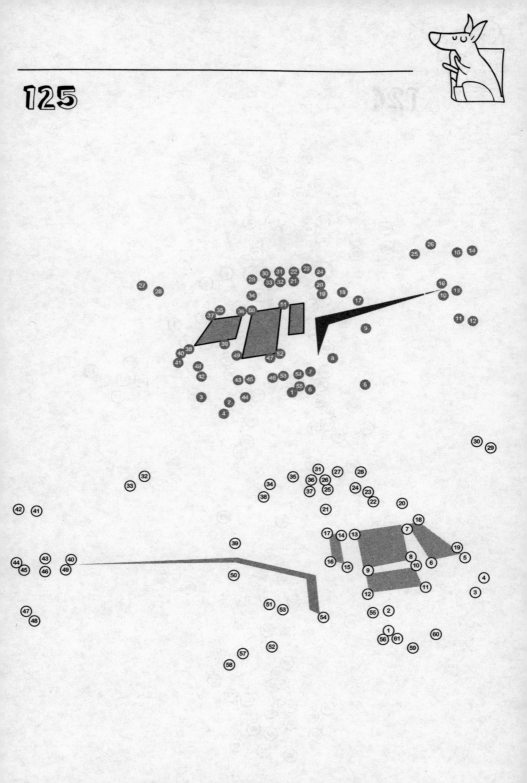

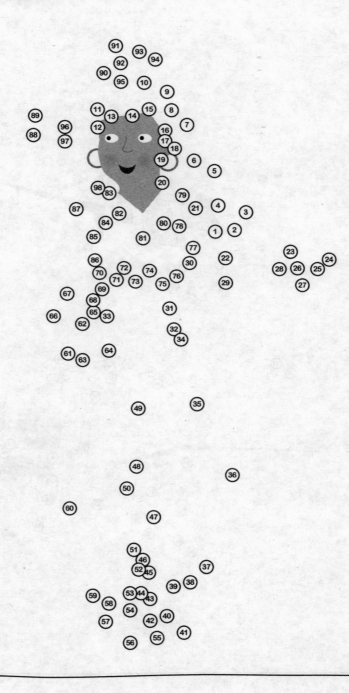

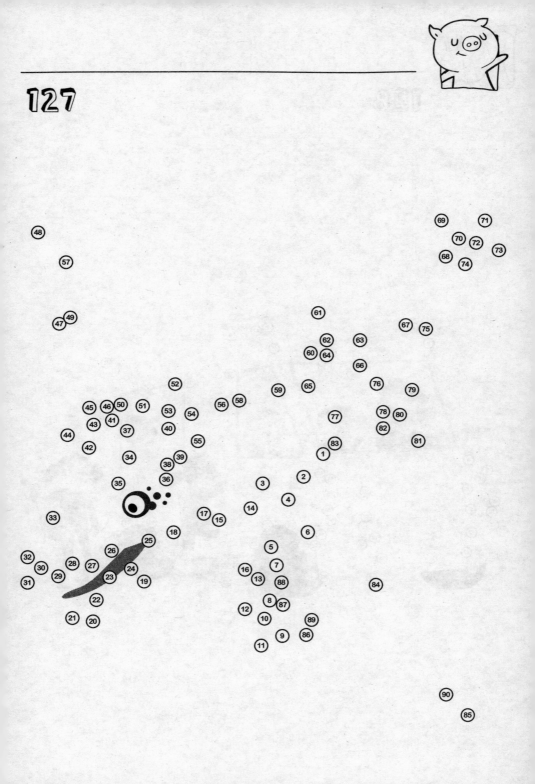

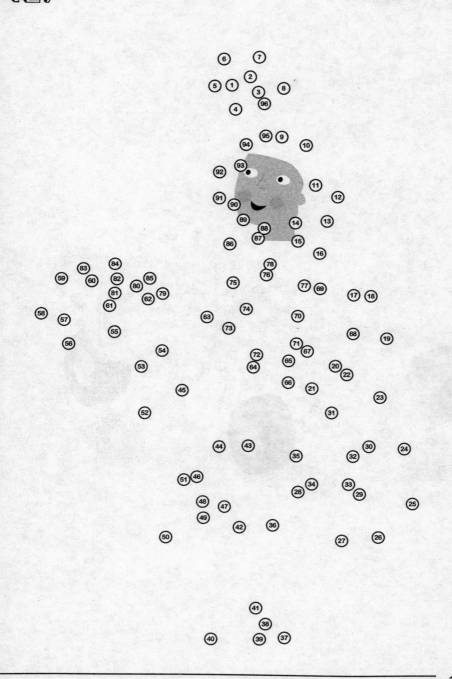

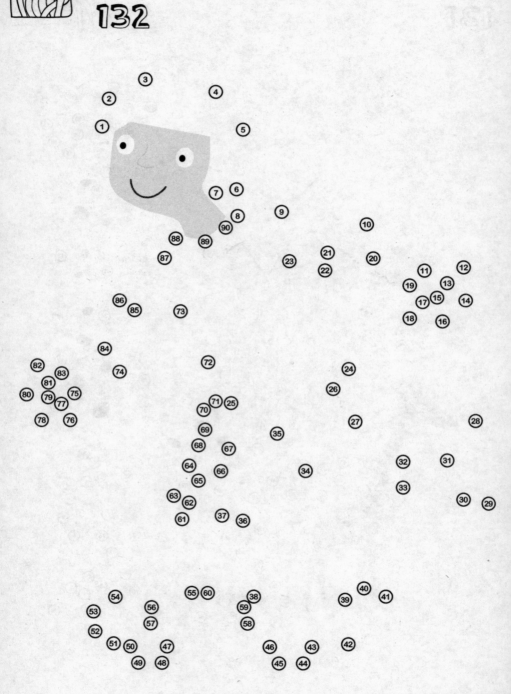

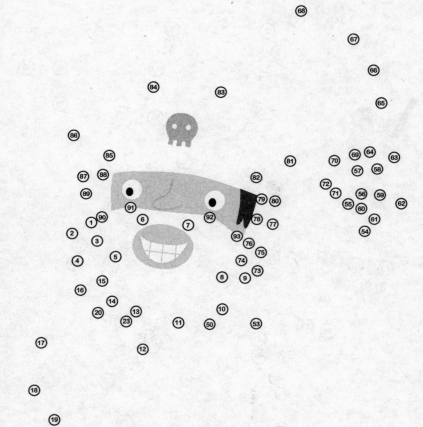

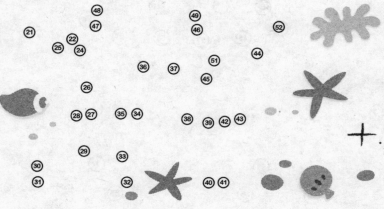

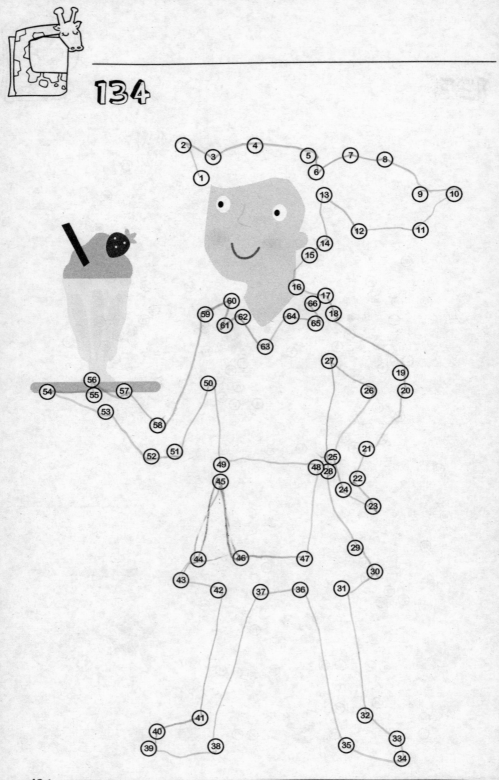

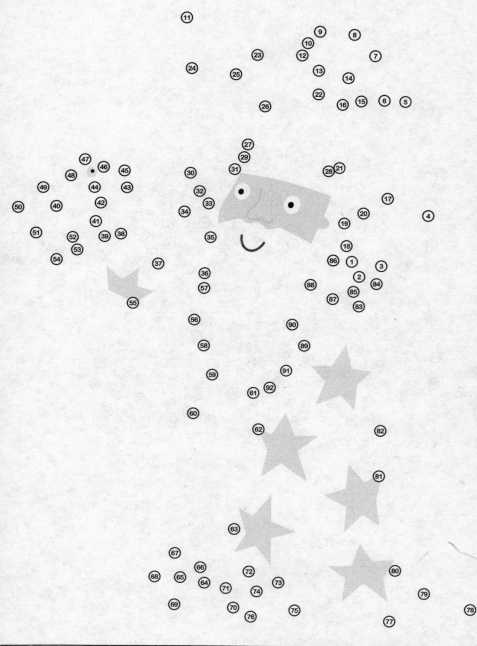

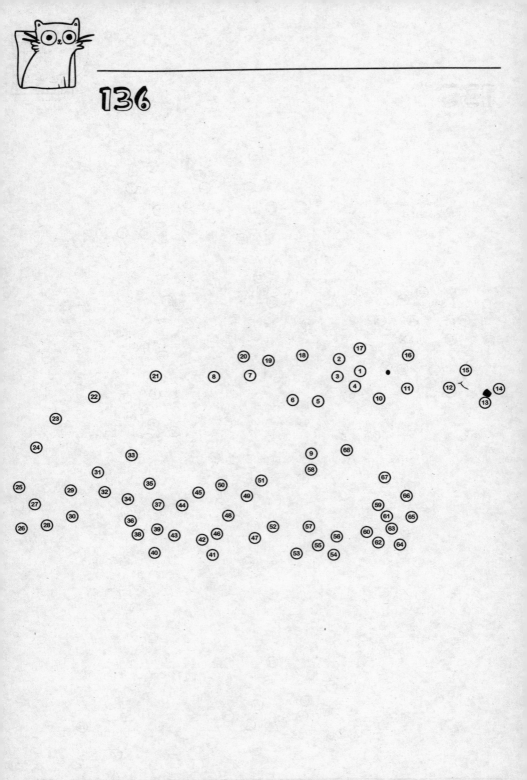

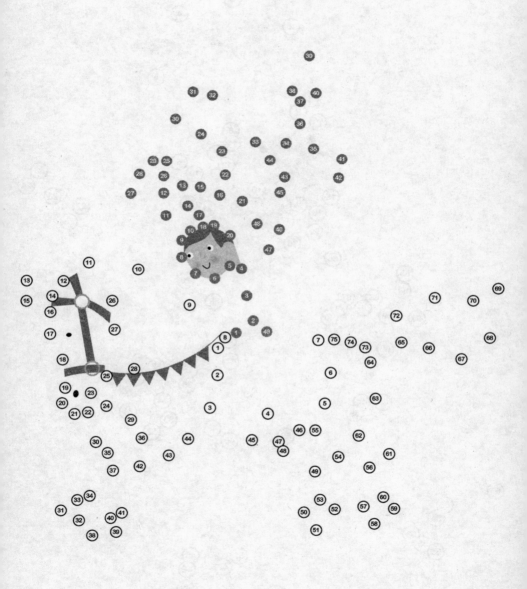

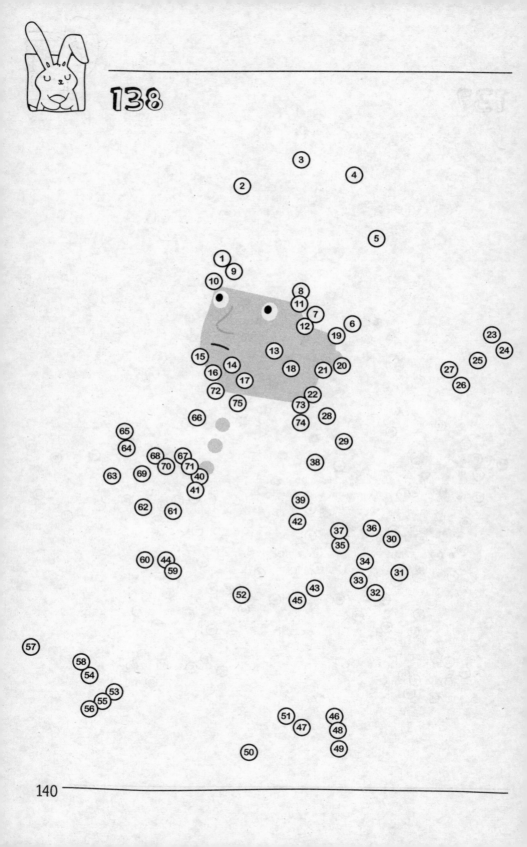

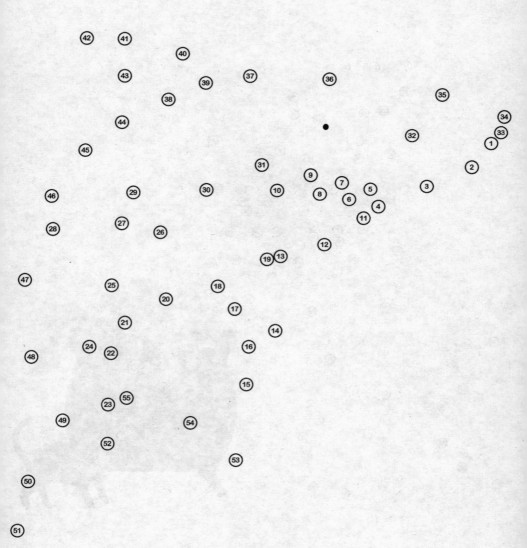

140

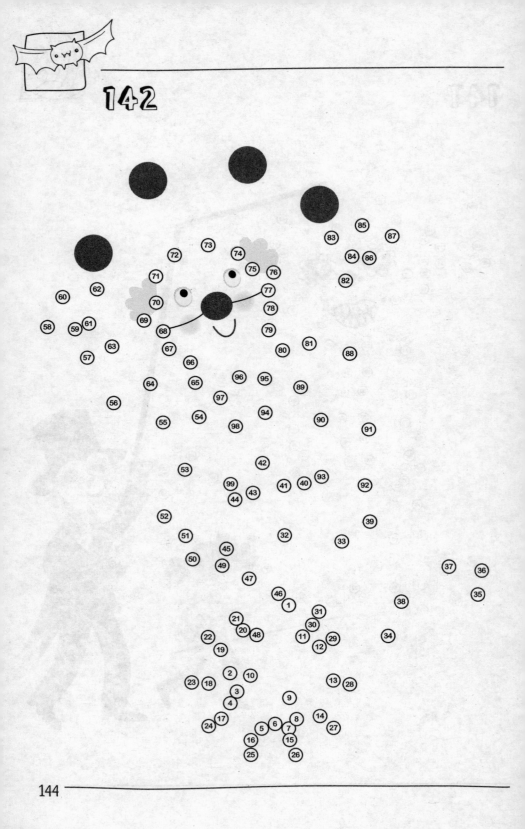

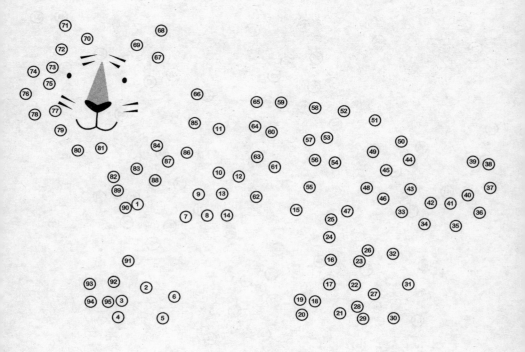

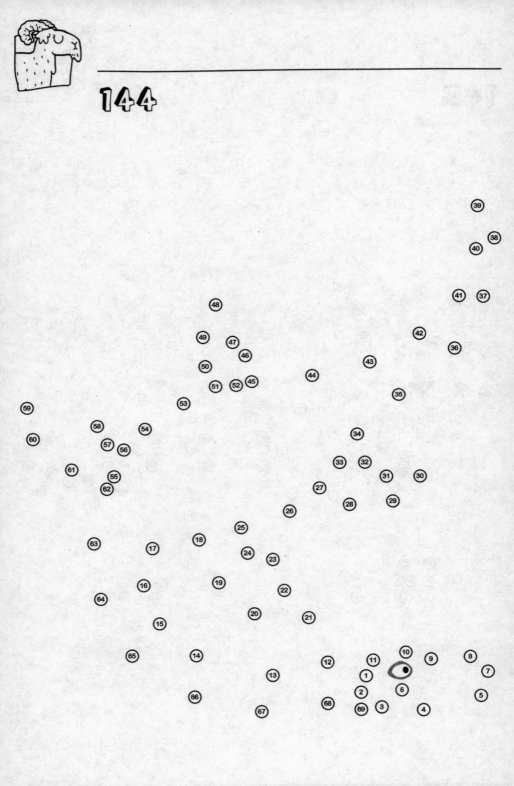

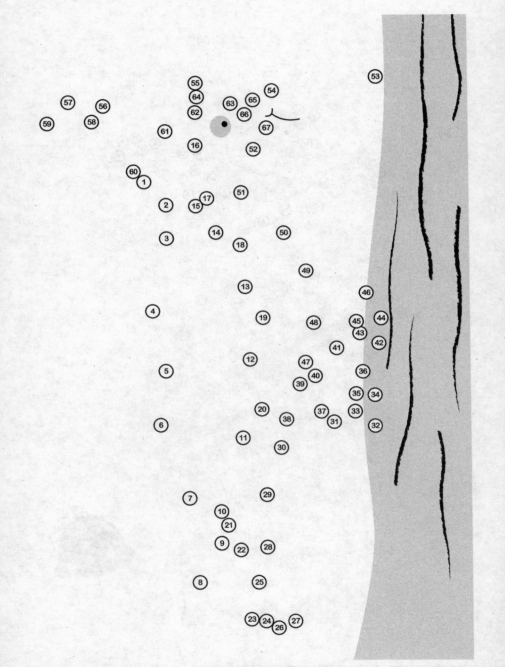

148

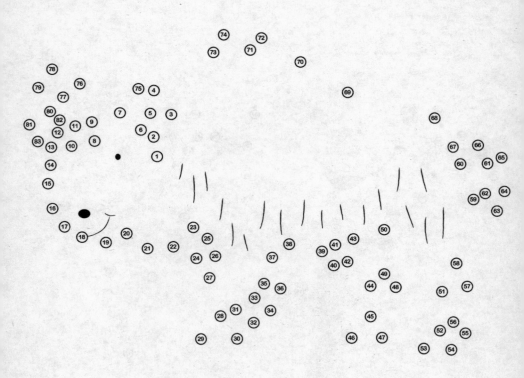

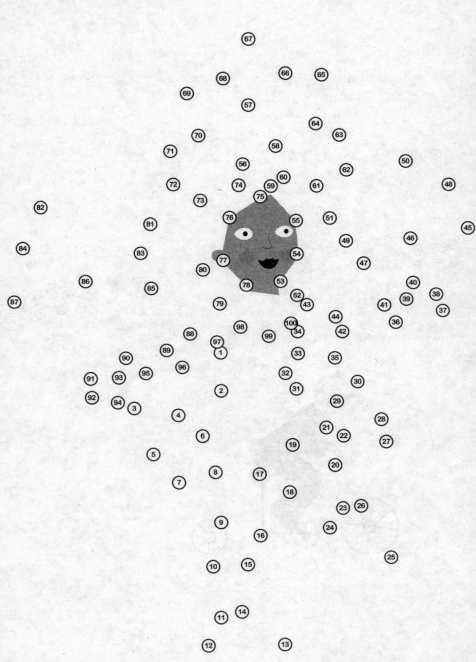

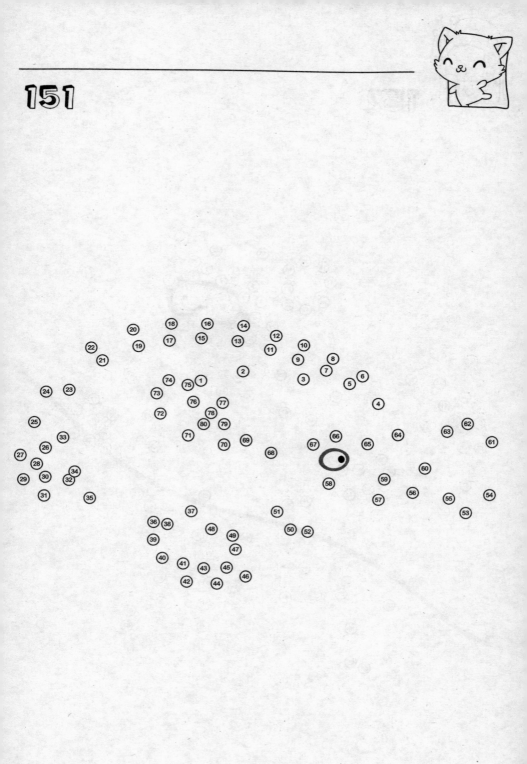

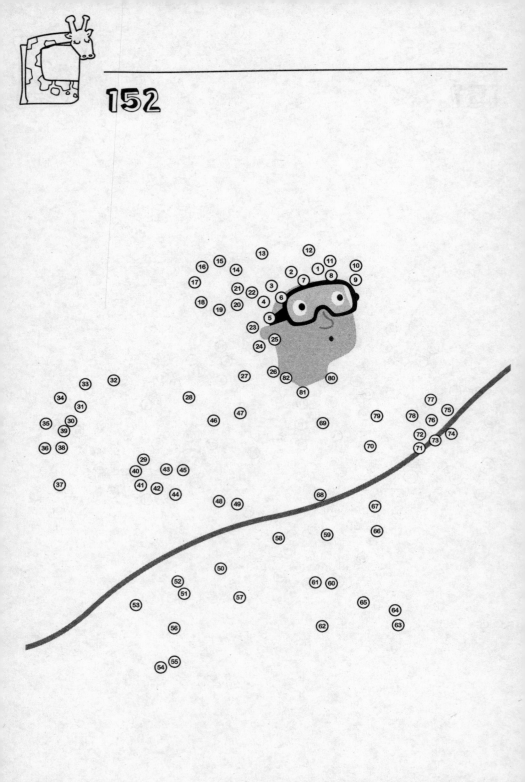

153

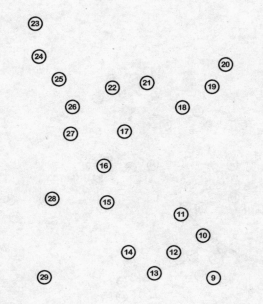

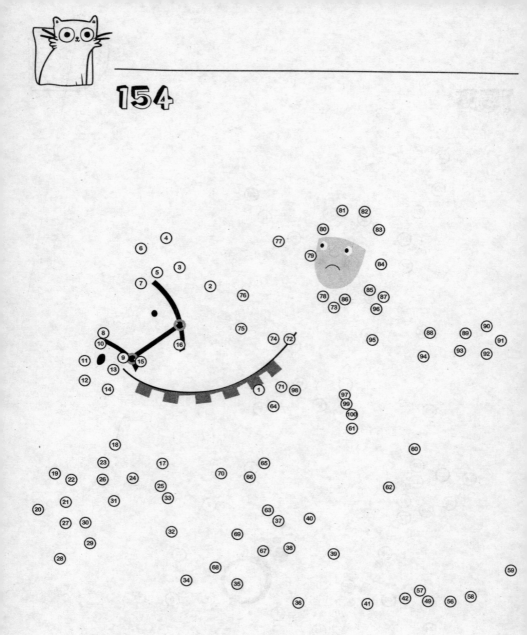

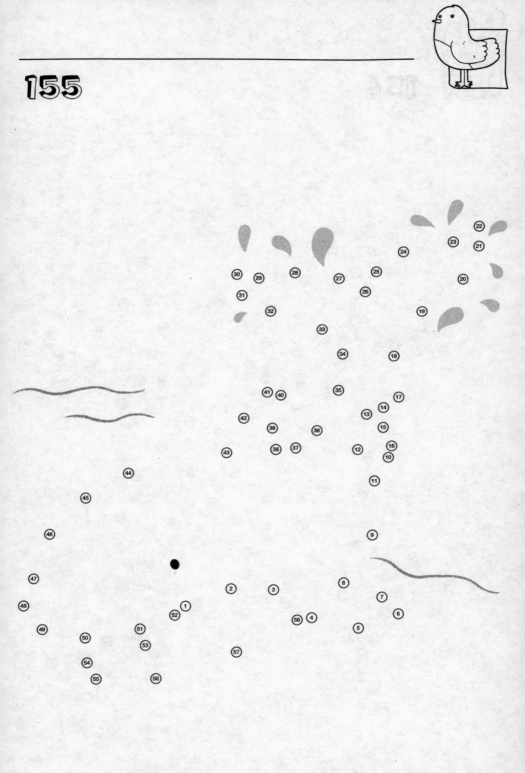

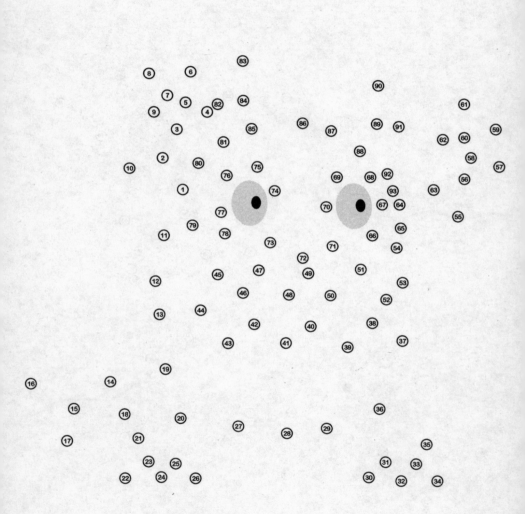

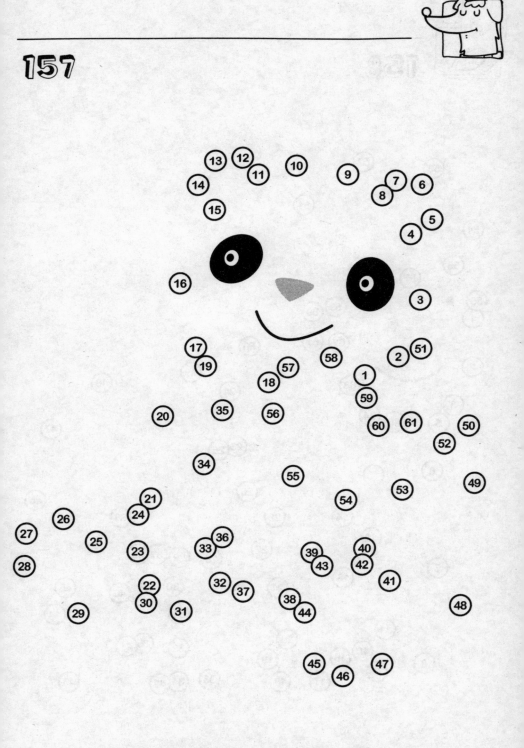

158

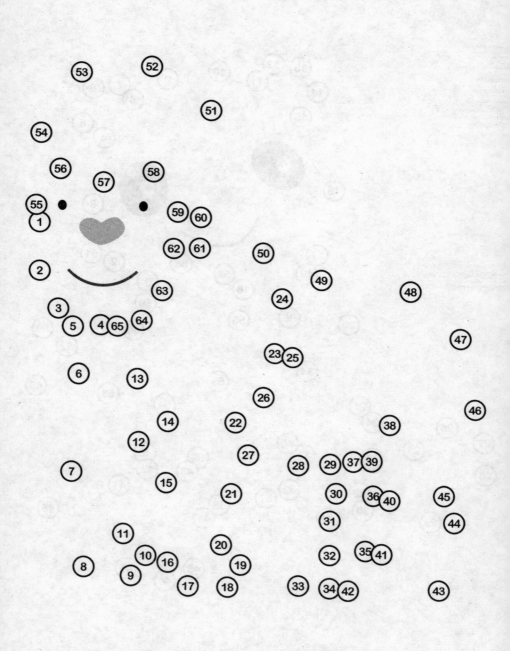

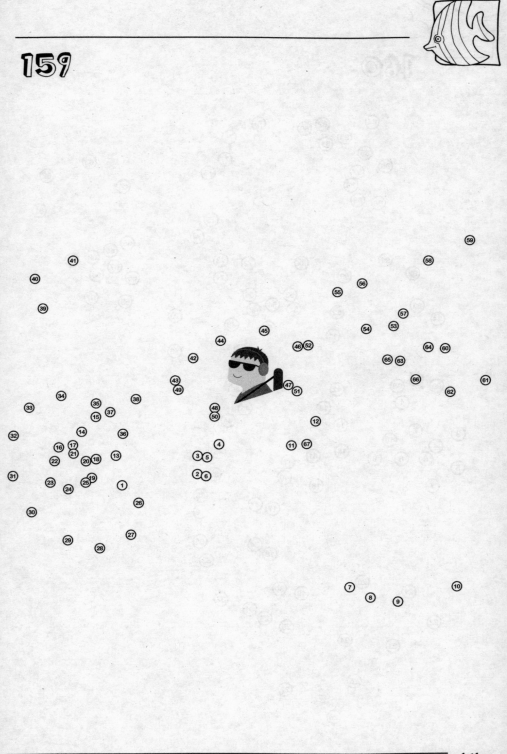

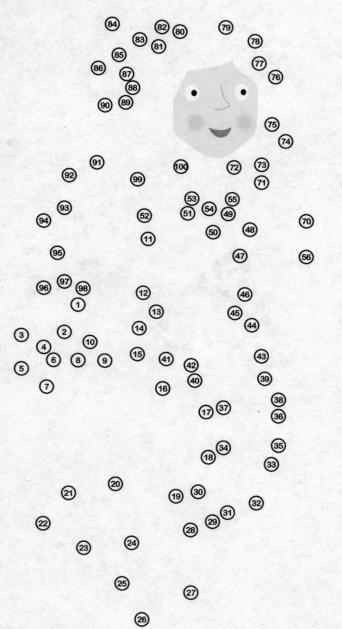

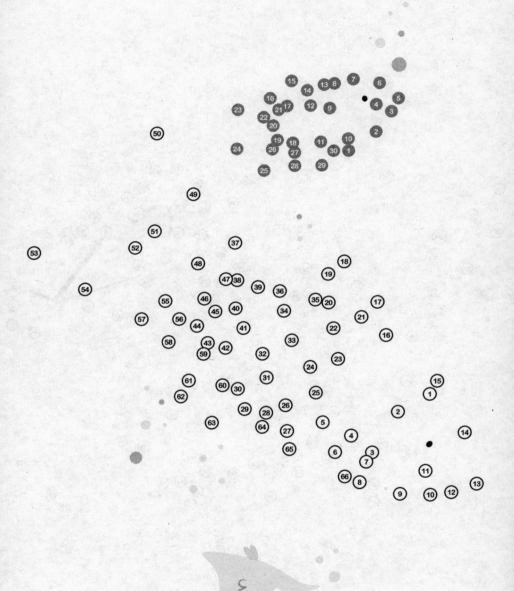

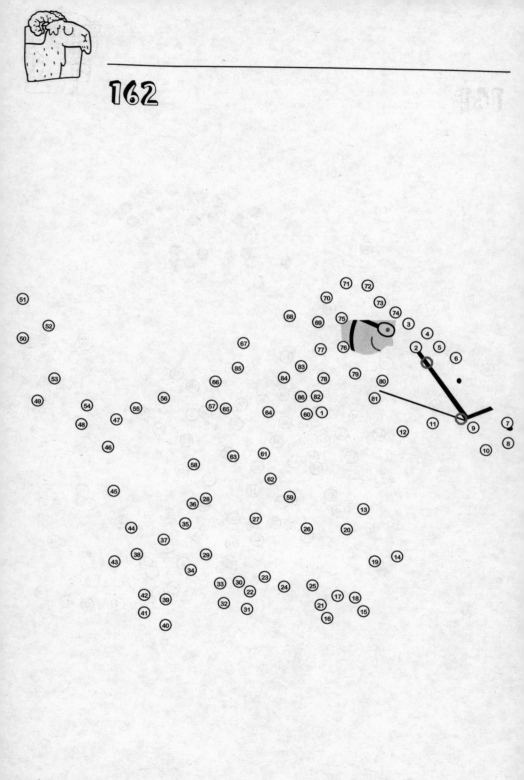

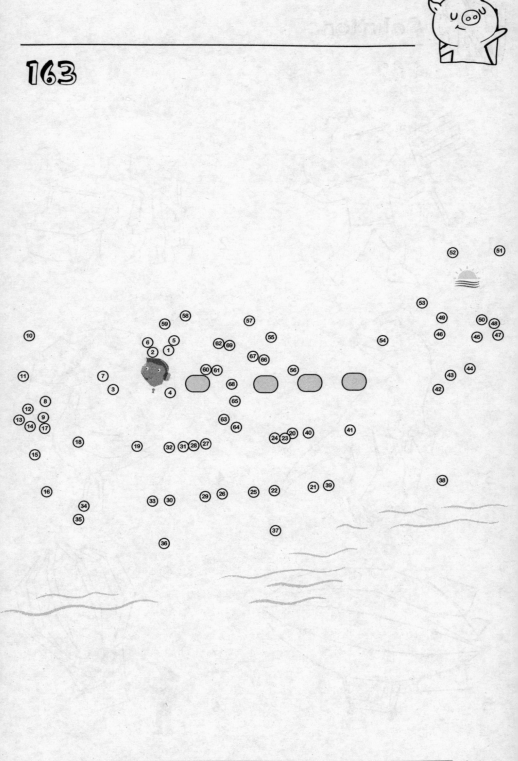

1

2

3

4

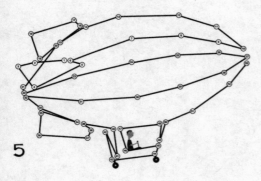

5

6

7

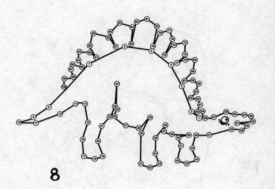

8

9

10

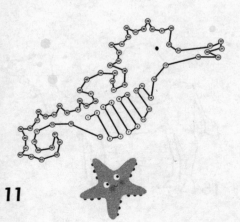

11

12

Solutions

13

14

15

16

17

18

19

20

21

22

23

24

Solutions

25

26

27

28

29

30

Solutions

31

32

33

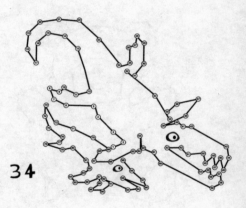

34

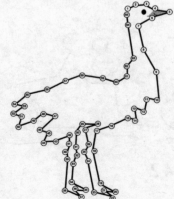

35

36

Solutions

37

38

39

40

41

42

Solutions

43

44

45

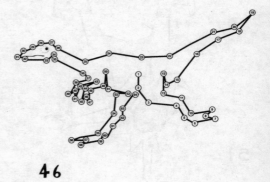

46

47

48

Solutions

49

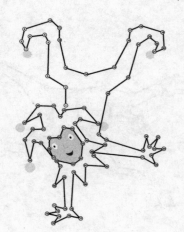

50

51

52

53

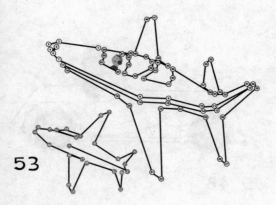

54

Solutions

55

56

57

58

59

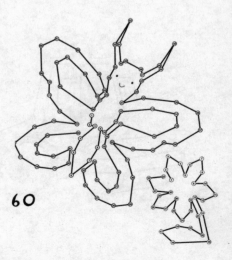

60

Solutions

61

62

63

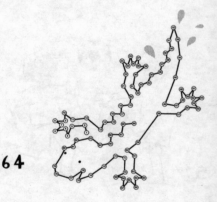

64

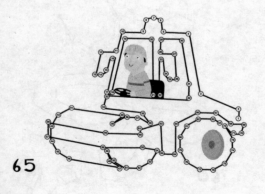

65

66

Solutions

67

68

69

70

71

72

73

74

75

76

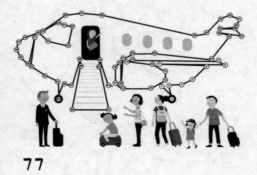

77

78

79

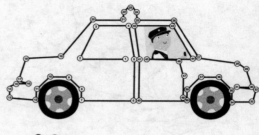

80

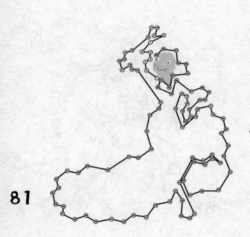

81

82

83

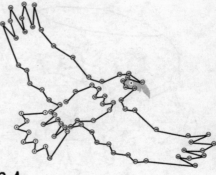

84

Solutions

85

86

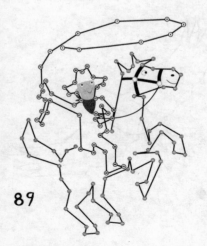

87

88

89

90

91

92

93

94

95

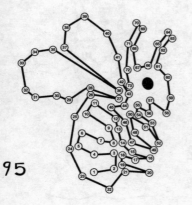

96

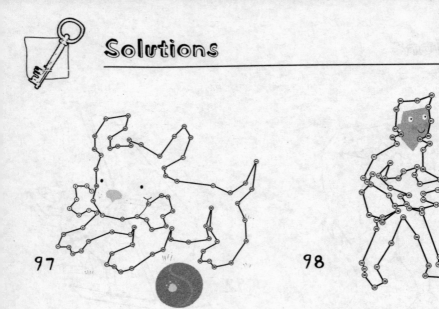

97

98

99

100

101

102

Solutions

103

104

105

106

107

108

109

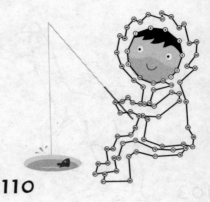

110

111

112

113

114

115

116

117

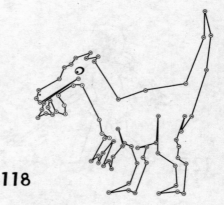

118

119

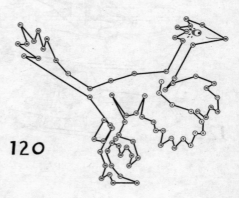

120

121

122

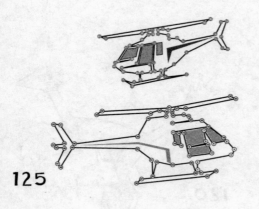

123

124

125

126

Solutions

127

128

129

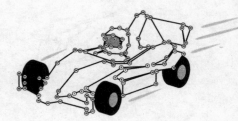

130

 131

132

Solutions

133

134

135

136

137

138

Solutions

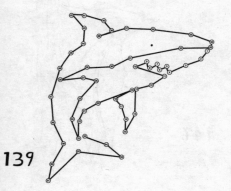

139

140

141

142

143

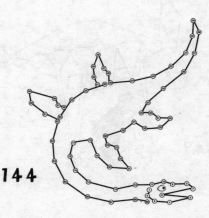

144

145

146

147

148

149

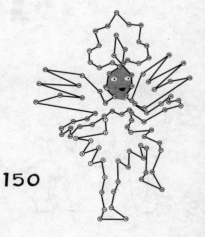

150

151

152

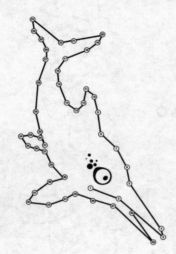

153

154

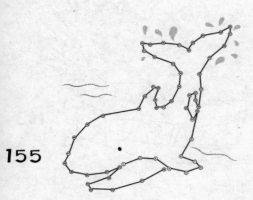

155

156

Solutions

157

158

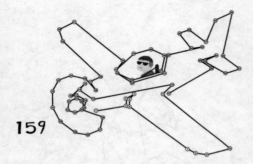

159

160

161

162

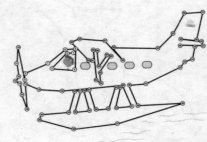

163